"A riveting experience, tears turned to laughter, and silent reflection. A canopy of freshness, a kaleidoscope of life's journey."

—Judith Ann Harris, Educator
Chicago, Illinois

"Love, heart, hope, and resilience emanates off the pages like few writers have the skill. Knowing the author gives me a greater understanding for her total persona, she is professional, strong, and fair with people."

—LTG (Ret'd) Paul E. Funk
Retired Army Commanding General

"For me, the story of Garland and Brian springs to life and into my consciousness because it is told with frank honesty by the woman who truly knows them best, their mother."

—Beverly White-Higgs, Journalist
Altadena, California

"The author, Myrtle L. Captain, probably has more to do with the smooth transition from segregation to desegregation in the Temple school system than any other single individual. To say that she is "bigger than life" would be an understatement. In this book, she bares her soul in a fashion very typical of her total commitment to the betterment of mankind. Her constant referral to God and love as the key ingredients to rearing children in a single parent family environment can only help every parent, no matter what their "status" in life. It has been my privilege to know two of her children, Garland and LaTrell. They are a masterpiece. This is a book for all times and, most certainly for all parents."

—Bob McQueen, AD/Head FB Coach, Temple ISD
Temple, Texas

"This book presents the strengths of the author under adverse circumstances. It demands respect for her as a single mother who never gave up and demonstrated resilience that made her family united survivors and victors."

—Jacqueline D. McClanahan, RN

"This book clearly depicts a single mother's power to make a positive transition through many eras. It shows her triumph and victories of having a close and personal spiritual connection and a relentless desire to overcome the obstacles she met in life."

—A.C. Sutton
Former President Texas State Conference of N.A.A.C.P.
Former Vice-President of National N.A.A.C.P. Board of Directors

"This story is told with honesty and without artifice. Parents and children can learn much from this book. I know Garland and respect him, but more so now that I have read this book."

—Rod Mullen, President & CEO
Amity Foundation of California, Porterville, CA

"The reader who cannot find something to whoop about in this book is not alive. It is filled with warm, funny, and touching anecdotes. The author's memoir reveals the innermost heart of a down to earth woman who stands fiercely by her family, faith, and values while still conveying the bewilderment and horror of modern-day conflict. One of her gifts lies in throwing human light on intolerable events. It combines the child's sense of wonder with adult intelligence and is written in some of the finest prose that exist in contemporary lifestyle."

—D. Lorimier, Warden II

"This book chronicles great love. The love of a Christian mother has allowed the author to honestly expose her trials and hardships to glorify the Lord and the power of faith."

—Raven Kazen, Director of Victim Services of Texas Department of Criminal Justice

THE WARDEN AND HIS BROTHER

THE WARDEN AND HIS BROTHER,

from Their Mother's Point of View

Myrtle L. Captain

Foreword by Tim West, Retired Warden—TDCJ

VANTAGE PRESS
New York

FIRST EDITION

Published by Vantage Press, Inc.
516 West 34th Street, New York, New York 10001

Manufactured in the United States of America
ISBN: 0-533-13046-8

Library of Congress Catalog Card No.: 98-91090

0 9 8 7 6 5 4 3 2

This book is dedicated to my children. Especially my youngest son, Garland and my oldest son, Brian. My daughter, Charmin LaTrell, is minimized only to stay focused on the title and purpose of this writing. In its sequel, *Twisted Fate* you will learn what a major role she has in our family and how very special she is to each of us. Garland encouraged me to write this book because he and his brother's love for each other and their bond, has survived the twisted fate of choosing different paths and has remained bonded. He titled it *The Warden and His Brother; From Their Mother's Point of View* because he knows I see beyond the immediate and usually my analytical views are different and of great value. He knows I am an analytical thinker and that I can find a good and positive learning experience in most all situations. Garland and Brian believe our life experiences have some healing and redeeming values for others with similar experiences.

My daughter, Charmin LaTrell, is our custodian of happiness and light hearted life. She is a pretty girl with her own set of specialties. She is my first born, and my only girl. I tried to ensure that her life was not filled with the anguish and pain that I experienced. Her brothers have always shown her love and have been protective of her person and character. I believe that a girl or woman should never be battered by any man. To that end I mandated that her brothers never strike her. I taught them to "put your hands in your pockets and call me."

My oldest son, Brian, is our custodian of joy. His potential far exceeded his performance. He knew this book would largely focus on many of his dark days. But, he also knew it would be educationally beneficial to anyone facing a dilemma or the twisted fate of siblings surviving different choices and overcoming major obstacles of life. From my point of view an aching heart can be hurt and healed by an honest self-reality check.

My youngest son, Garland, is our custodian of vision and wisdom. He knew writing this book would open some old wounds and release some haunting family secrets. From my point of view, personal freedom exist when our mental closets are free of haunting secrets.

I continually benefit from LaTrell's vibrant personality, Brian's joy and Garland's vision.

"If an idea develops into more than 100 pages of 12 pitch typed in double space print, it may be another book waiting to be written, printed and published. Seize the opportunity to share it with others through the printed word."

—Myrtle L. Captain

Contents

Foreword

This is a revealing book, one that opens the heart and soul of a loving family. The mother puts herself on display and undresses her life in such a way that few would have the courage to do. In doing so, she describes an era in history which most of us have an opinion about. Some condone, while others condemn. Those over forty may have strong personal feelings about this era and those younger can only accept what they have heard from those with the strong opinions.

The story moves quickly into the mother's dealings with her children and less with her own rearing. You must understand her, to understand the decisions she made, the love she gave up, the love she received, and the desire to provide a better life for her children. The interaction of all the family members is the important ingredient that binds this group of individuals together. It would be easy to point to parts of the story and make excuses for the performance or lack of performance of the different individuals. The story proves that love can overcome economic, social, cultural, genetic, and self imposed shortcomings.

You don't need to know the family well to understand the insights that this story portrays. The mother gives all for her children. The warden is considered by his peers as a "gentle giant" and the story will reveal his nature and spirit to all readers. The pressures created by the brother for him, helped both to grow. We must accept the consequences of our actions, but those consequences do not include rejection unless we choose it.

The reader will soon feel a theme in this book. At first you will think it is all about a family and what they overcame, but you will realize a different theme as the story develops. God is a forgiving God, a providing God, and a loving God.

Tim West
Retired Senior Warden of Mark Stiles Unit
of Texas Department of Corrections

Preface

This is the true story of a lady reared in a central Texas town of approximately 25,000 in population. It had some very distinct features typical of the climate of the times. She was born in 1939 and reared during the post-Depression years. The segregated lives of people in her community were strongly influenced by the segregated Army. The perils of segregated living patterns in America were also a part of her life. However, as a child she was not aware of what that meant, nor was she aware of why limitations were imposed upon her as an African American.

She did not understand why people in her community were fighting the evils of segregation, though she learned very young that there were things she could not do because of her race. For example, she knew not to go through the front door of a neighborhood Caucasian cafe to buy hamburgers for her family. She knew the cook was her neighbor, and she conversed with him as she patiently waited for hamburgers and exited by the back door and walked down the alley to her home, nearby. She was also a victim of the times when her father and other black people moved to California in search of a better living. Her mother's choice to remain in Temple was smart because her mother had the security of a nice mortgage-free home, a critical ingredient for survival.

The struggling times of the thirties and forties

brought much stress to all families. Life for blacks living near an Army post was impacted because of blatant discrimination against the black soldiers and their families. The segregated USOs provided sheltered entertainment for black soldiers but the gambling shacks, bootlegged liquor, prostitution, and night clubs provided other than sheltered fun. The author's childhood was spent at the front line of others' unsavory living. She was not impressed by hustlers nor hustling; instead, she sought life's options from her neighborhood church family. Neighborhood civic needs and activists attracted her childhood attention and she also felt a need to help improve her community. She addressed the city library's racism at the age of thirteen and made a positive difference.

Her young adult life was encircled by the military community and made way for her to become another generation of the same cycle. She rebelled and opted for better chances in life for herself and her children in the '60s. She defied the norms of her culture and succeeded in ways that were not designed for blacks. Her success story with her children defies all the odds of her time.

Her power to overcome family dysfunctionalism and discrimination in her life and career is to be applauded. She and her children's lives are no different than that of many young parents of today. The beauty of her story is that she overcame many events and traumas that dumbfounded others. Despite life's trials, she made great contributions to her family, to society in her central Texas community, the state of Texas, the United States of America and the world. This book and the success of her life have been proven un-time restricted. It is food and medicine for all people and all times.

Background

Garland, a senior warden in the Texas Department of Corrections, owns the original idea for this book. He wanted it to be helpful for families who have the twisted fate of siblings traveling different paths and their bonds not being destroyed. He had little idea that my brother and I shared the same twisted fate as he and his brother, but we never bonded. Fortunately, the bond of the subjects of this text (Brian and Garland) began with my pregnancy of the warden and has never been broken. From their mother's (my) point of view nothing can be more valuable than a brother's and sister's love for each other. Thanks be to God for their bond.

My brother Boonie and I were reared in a single-parent home. Our father moved to California before my birth, in search for work. Our mother, Ruby, rented rooms to supplement her income from laundry work. She is known by her first name, Ruby, by her choice. My brother and I grew up simply coexisting as sister and brother. We were never taught to love each other. However, I love my brother because the whole family loved him and expected me to love him, too, despite his abuse of me. From my point of view, siblings must be *taught* to love each other. It doesn't happen by osmosis.

The readers of this book and its sequel, *Twisted Fate,* should find relief in knowing that persons united by God can coexist and mature together, lead separate lives and yet never bond. God allows people the independent right to love and care for whom they please, including parents and their children, siblings and other relatives. However, whatever God wills, will be done. I thank God for that divine realization.

THE WARDEN AND HIS BROTHER

1

My Twisted Fate

There was no way but down for me to go. Hatred, hostility and abuse were my only frame of reference. My brother went to school at the age of four. My mother said Professor Sampson, the colored school principal, came through the neighborhood, saw him playing, and stopped and talked to him. When Professor Sampson asked my mother, "Why isn't that boy in school?" she expressed that he was only four years of age. The principal had noticed that he was smart and could learn, so he enrolled my brother in school, where he was placed with children two and more years older than himself. He thought he was their age and tried to prove he was equally or more mature. Going to school so young made him mentally and socially much more than six years older than me.

At a young age, my brother became a leader of mischief. He was known in school for not only being smart but also disobedient and disrespectful to his teachers. He told Mrs. O. T. Pannell that he wanted to go to every major penitentiary in the USA. She called Ruby. Ruby came to school and whipped him in the classroom. It embarrassed him so bad that he was no longer the kingpin of his class. After that incident he lost all interest in going to school because he was ridiculed by his friends about the awesome whipping he received from his mother in front of his classmates. Today, when his friends remind him of that whipping, he gets angry as if it was yesterday. Childhood embarrassments hurt forever.

As a teenager, my brother stole from the neighborhood grocery and drug stores. He liked criminal activities. He was impressed by the wild life things that were available to us through the traffic of renters in our home. He saw bad and illegal things as glamorous and was in a hurry to show his manhood in the wild life scene. I saw the same things my brother saw and was never impressed. I detested everything I saw and lived with.

My brother's stealing led to many other things: drinking cheap wine, smoking cigarettes, smoking marijuana, and selling and using illegal drugs. Over a span of time, it netted him three trips to prisons and countless stays in city and county jails. His conduct and misbehavior spilled onto me. Many parents did not want me to play with their children because I was the sister of the bad boy. I understood their thoughts but I hated being held accountable for his actions. I hated being the sister of the bad boy and I hated being penalized for his conduct. Yet, I paid debts to society that my brother owed. And he made my coping with his problems more painful because he was always physically and mentally abusive to me, too, which I never understood because I loved him so much. Today, I don't worry about what I don't understand and am not responsible for. My mother's verbal abuse and negativism toward me led him to be even more physically violent and abusive to me. Clearly we never bonded as brother and sister.

Our relationship was too important a lesson for me to not pass on to my own children. I taught my sons never to strike each other nor their sister. I taught my sons, if their sister made them angry enough to hit her, to put their hands in their pockets and call me. From a mother's point of view, I taught my children to value, to respect, to love, to care for and to protect each other. I owed it to my children to break the vicious cycle of family violence and sibling rivalry and abuse.

As time passed, my brother moved to Los Angeles, California and quickly joined the wild and rough life of a "hustler." When he came back and forth to Temple, he came to see "his momma." I never thought he came to see me. Each time he came home, our mother would pit us against each other all over again. For me that was a never-ending saga, an accepted way of life. In California, my brother managed bars, gambling halls, and ran wild women for hire. He physically abused his women, too. It seems my brother never had either respect or regard for women, including me, his only sister. Many of his women "for hire" loved him more with each beating. I never understood women loving abusive men.

I stayed in Temple because I never desired to leave. I was active and participated in events at Mount Zion Missionary Baptist Church and Dunbar schools. I became one of Reverend and Mrs. C. S. Williamson's favorite children. Rev. Williamson was a stern, but fair, no-nonsense man, and his lovely wife was the epitome of a preacher's wife, citizen, and a good Christian. I went with them on many church trips, and through them I learned there were options in life. Once, I heard my mother say, "I'm not like some people who lie and say my child is pretty. I know Myrt Louise is not pretty so I dress her well to make her look decent." That was an awful and stinging statement but I learned to capitalize on her thoughts; I used my ugliness to get my mother to buy the best clothing and prettiest of accessories to make me look like I was a preacher's daughter.

My features and dark skin had no bearing when I was with Rev. and Mrs. Williamson. Because he was dark and she was lighter, I blended well between their complexions. Some people thought I was their natural daughter, until I became an adult. Mrs. Williamson and I laughed when people said I looked like my father, meaning Rev. C. S. Williamson. We always corrected them; we refused to lie by deception or omission. I worked hard to please Rev. and Mrs. Williamson and to become the Secretary of Sunday School and Vacation Bible School. Becoming the Sunday School Secretary filled my need to be like Brooksie Nell McGarity. During vacation Bible School, Rev. Williamson complimented me by saying, "You are going to be a good business woman; no one has accurately predicted how much block ice we need for the next day." Perhaps his compliment gave me the sense of self value which has lasted the whole of my lifetime.

When my brother did not live in Temple, it took many dark clouds off my head and shoulders and a serious weight off my heart. During his absence, I was not ridiculed for being the "bad boy's sister." His absence opened many closed chambers in my mind and heart. I was free. I learned to love being alone, I was responsible for only me.

In school I always studied hard to make good grades, because I thought people only liked smart and pretty people. I accepted not being pretty but knew I could study and be smart. When my brother did not live in Temple most of my friends' parents treated me as an individual. I was happy when people did not treat me as if I was as bad as my brother's reputation.

In the eighth grade I wanted, competed for, and earned the position of Head Majorette for Dunbar High School's pep squad. I won and kept that position from the ninth grade through my senior year and graduation. My brother was teased because his ugly little sister was a majorette and performed like a little show pony. I was proud despite my features. That position satisfied my need to be like Essie Mae Reddic. She was a very pretty dark-skinned girl, loved by everyone and smart, and I wanted to be exactly like her, I became a good imposture. My mother saw me perform at only one game out of four years of performances. I became immune to the pain of not having my mother present to share my successes. I learned to be happy with whoever was there and stroked me. I participated and excelled in many different school activities and also became rather popular.

While a teenager, I became civically interested and organized the Southside Progressive Teenagers Club, of which my neighborhood friends were members. Our club studied inequities and pressured the city government for change. I, personally, addressed segregation in the Temple Public Library over an Emily Post book of Etiquette. My mother bought me a copy for Christmas to keep me from pursuing the issue with the Temple Public Library. As a club we addressed and corrected poor park facilities. We fought and won battles for Negro teenagers. We hosted chaperoned lawn parties, one of the major social outlets for children of our age.

My brother dropped out of school early and I graduated from Dunbar High School in May of 1957 as an honor student. To me this was an achievement to be envied. I worked hard to graduate and studied hard to become an honor student. My senior uncle James Flake flew from Los Angeles, California to attend my high school graduation ceremony. I was proud and grateful for his presence. It made me feel that he loved me. Somehow, it also told me that my father would have come, if he were alive. My mother made Uncle James late for our graduation ceremony and he was angry. He did not know that without him she might not have been there at all. I received several awards that night. The most coveted one, in my opinion, was the Hornsby Homemaking Award, which was the preeminence of success. My graduation was a happy experience and a major accomplishment, though it meant nothing to my mother and my brother. In retrospect, neither my mother nor my brother graduated from high school. Maybe my graduation spawned maternal and sibling envy? Uncle James could not understand why my mother treated my graduation so lightly. He never knew that none of my accomplishments meant anything to my mother. Uncle James was wrathful and held his lateness against my mother for years. In response to his anger she just laughed as if it was meaningless.

After my high school graduation the roads of my brother and I took a wider turn from each other. I went to Prairie View A & M College in pursuit of a degree in homemaking. I dreamed of earning a Ph.D. and being the dean of a Homemaking Department in a leading college or university. After entering Prairie View, I learned that I was pregnant. Being pregnant meant that my education had come to an end, and I felt all of my future plans would come to a screeching halt. I thought, at last my mother could truthfully say that I was a total failure and was no better than my criminally mind brother. Having a child out of wedlock, at that time, would have been considered proof that I was a good-for-nothing. In the minds of those who did not wish me well, it was confirmation of their belief; I was unfit for society.

I was terribly unhappy during my pregnancy. I thought my lover would be happy when I told him that I was carrying his baby, but I was rudely awakened when he told me, "I can't take care of a baby, I got my car to take care of." Those words made me feel I was drowning in a big deep sea of disappointment and deception. I could not visualize how to get out of that situation! I told him, "You take care of your car and I will take care of my baby." During my entire pregnancy, my mother was both physically and mentally abusive to me; everyday was confrontational. I kept wondering *why is his car more important than my being pregnant with his baby?* Cars still have more of a priority to young men than the more important things of life.

My mother made a neighbor's son my brother's replacement and used him to further her abuse on me. He was the new king of our house, another thing I could not understand.

My stepfather, Sgt. Archie Lee Hicks, tried to fill in the gap for me. Hicks frequently told my mother not to do nor say cruel things to me. He treated me nicely, and tried to protect me from the pain of my mother's mental and physical rages.

Hicks was a wonderful man. He took us to Austin to cash some insurance policies. He wanted to pay for the delivery of my baby. That made me happy. He also cashed two other policies. We were on the fifth floor of the insurance building. As we rode the elevator to the first floor my mother had taken all three checks and placed them in her purse. Hicks never knew that she kept all but the $50.00 down payment on my baby's birth. I paid the remainder of the bill after I got a job. That also confused me. Why did she take the money Hicks had provided for me to deliver my baby? Another unresolved pain.

2

Charmin LaTrell's Birth

On April 21, 1958, I delivered my first little bundle of love, Charmin LaTrell Flakes at Cora Anderson Negro Hospital, a unit of Scott and White Hospital. My baby remained in the hospital about ten days after me because of a respiratory problem. I had time to think about our future. I knew I needed a job so I asked Mrs. Hines and Mrs. Hall, our neighbors and long time friends, to help me get a job at the laundry at Fort Hood, which they did. Charmin LaTrell was five weeks and six days old, being voluntarily kept by my mother while I worked the night shift. Soon my mother said I owed her a specified amount of money for keeping my baby. She charged me more than I could afford. I only earned sixty-eight cents per hour. I had to pay for my ride, buy food for both my baby and me, pay my mother rent for staying in the room she had built with my money that was reserved for my education through my deceased father's Navy benefits. I was burdened beyond my belief.

I was excited to get a job at Fort Hood's laundry. I knew decent paying work in Temple was very scarce, especially for Negro women. Domestic work was prevalent. I never wanted to do domestic work for white women on the north side of town; it appeared too racially degrading. I knew black women who worked for years for white families and had to walk home late in the evening to take care of their own families. I knew that such labor did not pay enough to take care of my little family and offered no benefits. There were some white women who drove their employees home and the employee had to sit in the back seat because the front seat was occupied by a dog or cat. They appeared to perch up in the front seat like a human. That looked like a serious lack of respect for the worthiness of their employee. I swore I would never accept being treated less than anyone's dog or cat.

I wanted and began to look for Mr. Right to take me out of my lonesome misery.

3

Meeting Mr. Right Soldier and Brian's Birth

I knew the single women working at Fort Hood's laundry planned to meet Mr. Right Soldier. I hoped that I would, too. I wanted to get away from my mother, and I believed that marrying would resolve my problems. One Sunday afternoon while my mother and I drove through South Eighth Street, I caught a glimpse of the most handsome, bright-eyed man I had ever seen. Later that evening I went to the Night Hawk nightclub with some friends. I was asked to dance by a man I thought I had seen somewhere but I knew I did not know him. He seemed familiar; we danced and danced, he held me while we waited for the next song. He made me feel so special. He complimented my appearance, the smell of my perfume, my personality, and admired my shapely body. I loved his attention. God knew I was hungry for acceptance by someone special. I was vulnerable because I had just come out of the depths of rejection by my sweetheart. My friends left me at the night club and the very handsome gentleman offered to take me home. As we walked to his beautiful jet black Oldsmobile Delta Super 88, I felt faint. He was the guy I had seen earlier that day. I wondered could this be my dream man or Mr. Right Soldier.

We dated for eleven months and thoroughly enjoyed each other's companionship. He became Mr. Right Soldier and my knight in shining armor. He was transferred from Fort Hood to Fort Carson, Colorado and sent for me to come to Colorado Springs, Colorado to become his bride. I went to Colorado Springs and became his bride. It did not take long for my knight's shining armor to start rusting. He became mean and very physically violent to me. After a nasty fight, I did defend myself, we signed divorce papers on the grounds of *me* being physically and mentally abusive to *him*. The truth was quite the contrary. I came home. My mother again abused me and always spoke condescendingly to me. She laughed at me for my failed marriage. I looked for work, but I was too embarrassed to go back to Fort Hood's laundry. Mr. Right Soldier called and promised he would not be mean to me and wanted me to return to Colorado Springs, CO. I did. We got along much better. Against his will, I went to work at Fort Carson's laundry. Later I became pregnant with our baby. He acted as though he was happy to become a father. We planned how we would take care of our unborn. He suggested I come home to have our baby at Fort Hood and save some money for his next duty station. I agreed, that was a good idea. And I came home.

Shortly after I was home, I received the finalized divorce papers we had initiated on my first return trip. I was not pregnant then; now I was. I was crushed. I could not understand why he abandoned me and our unborn child. In January I was rehired to work in the Fort Hood laundry. Some of the vicious women in the laundry began to humiliate me about my failed marriage. My mother and others said I was too ugly for him to ever have loved me. That hurt. He called and tried to intimidate and threaten me by saying the Army would press charges against me for not returning my identification card. He said the military police would come to my home and get the identification card from me. I ignored him and kept the card. I still have that identification card! It represents a time of my life that should have been happy. Despite the humiliation of my failed marriage I worked at the laundry and withstood the ridicule of my coworkers. I saved my money and prepaid for my baby's delivery at Dr. William J. Bruce's clinic. The divorce, however, prevented me from being privileged to deliver our baby at Fort Hood's Army hospital, at no cost. Some suggested God was mad at me and had sent these problems into my life. I did not believe God was mad at me and made plans for Brian's birth.

From my point of view I did not owe Mr. Right Soldier any information nor communication about my unborn child. Divorcing me while I was pregnant meant that he forfeited all of his rights as a father and for his son to share his surname.

Brian's Birth

Working among women who humiliated me for my failed marriage was difficult. Though I was scorned, I took pride in my appearance and held my head erect. I bought remnants of pretty fabric and made myself plenty of pretty maternity clothing. I looked better than many married mothers-to-be. I demonstrated the pride I gained by being presented with the Hornsby Homemaking Award. I was a "Hornsby Girl" and possessed an Eagle's mentality. I worked hard and ironed production daily. No one could accuse me of using my pregnancy to avoid carrying my load of the work for which I was being paid. Supervisors admired my stamina. Naysayers could not defeat me.

On May 13, 1960 I went to Dr. Bruce's clinic for a checkup. I told Dr. Bruce that I wanted to deliver my baby on Tuesday, May 17, 1960, because LaTrell had been born April 21st, a Monday. After my check-up Dr. Bruce asked if I could hold my baby until May 17th. I replied, yes. On Tuesday, May 17, 1960 I returned to the clinic and Dr. Bruce induced my labor and I was ready to deliver Brian. While in Dr. Bruce's clinic, I had labor pains and whistled. The nurses panicked; they thought my whistling was the out-of-order warning of the air-conditioning unit. I had asked Dr. Bruce to order me a boy when he ordered his babies. He laughed and said, "I'll order you a boy," and wrote "boy" on my folder. When Brian was born we cheered. My prayers were answered; I had a boy who looked like his dad. I named him Brian for a boy baby I had seen on television. I knew God was not mad at me because he stayed with me through the birth of this healthy and precious little boy. After his birth, I went home to my lonely bedroom and Charmin LaTrell.

That night, Della Reese sang on television. Della's melodious voice captured my attention and the words of her song seemed as though they were designed with me in mind. As she sang, her words ripped my heart into shreds. I cried as she sang:

> I know someday you are going to want me,
> When I'm in love with somebody new,
> Although you don't want me now,
> Oh! I'll get along somehow
> And then I won't want you."

Tears gushed profusely from my eyes; uncontrollably

I cried. I cannot forget that experience. Today I can sing those stinging words, at will. I wondered, *why did life continue to deal me such a bad hand, as in cards.* I could not remember anything I had done to anyone which compared to my pains. I feared, maybe, God was mad at me. Yet, I could only lean on and trust in God. Some people still tried to make me think God was mad at me and that was what had caused my life to run amuck. I thought that I could not get my life straight. But Rev. Williamson had taught me to have faith in God, so I called on God for comfort, and He delivered. I looked at little Brian, so pretty and healthy. Though it hurt, I knew Brian was the only precious gift I got from my failed marriage to Mr. Right Soldier. I shunned Rev. Williamson. I thought he was ashamed of me, too.

From my point of view, my son was a perfect little bundle of love. He had his daddy's big bright eyes and bowlegs, the features that I loved of Mr. Right Soldier who turned into Mr. Bad Soldier. I thanked God for His presence in my life, for my baby's good health and for my healthy delivery. When I looked at Brian, he was so innocent, I knew God was not mad at me, either.

I spent hours mentally sorting through my thoughts for directing my future. My stay with my mother, again was becoming worse. I knew I had to move into my own home. When my brother visited from California, he and my mother brought wrath deep into the depths of my very soul. His visits were disastrous for me.

4

My Brother's Visit From Los Angeles

My mother was so happy to see and have my brother visiting at 511 South Seventeenth Street. One Sunday afternoon, my brother came into the house while I was preparing food for my grandmother, Myrtle Lillie Williams, my children and me. My grandmother was extra hungry and my mother was visiting and eating at Aunt Betty's home. I asked Lillie to please be patient while I prepared the food. My brother heard me and went to Aunt Betty's house and told my mother I was cursing and abusing Lillie. They stormed into the kitchen and my brother proceeded to beat me, unmercifully, as if I was one of his whores on the streets. My mother stood and looked. I fell between the stove and sink. While falling I picked up a knife. My mother screamed, "Don't you cut my son in his face!" I knew it was time for me to move. I found solace in Aunt Betty.

My mother had told me our family was "us (she and Boonie) and you (me)." When I saw my mother encouraging my brother to beat me, I knew my mother meant it was them against me. I went to Aunt Betty's and used her telephone. Aunt Betty comforted and nursed my emotional wounds and the soreness in my body from the blows of my brother's fists. I hurt all over. I learned of a vacant apartment in the Vamp next door to one of my favorite childhood girlfriends, Ruby Dee. She offered to keep my children while I worked. God could not have been mad at me. I moved in the following Tuesday, using some of my savings for a down payment on furniture. Mr. Bush at J. T. Mayes Furniture Company believed in my character, and sold me new and good furniture on credit. My children's first bedroom suite was made by Bassett. I knew Bassett was quality furniture. I set up house in our small shotgun apartment in the Vamp.

The Vamp was considered as unsavory. The duplex shotgun apartments covered a block square. Each duplex had two front rooms, one small closet, a kitchen, a sinkless shower with commode. Most of the tenants were single mothers and families with plenty of children. Most of the single mothers did not work and received some form of welfare or governmental assistance. The adjoining backyards were square shaped with clotheslines. When the children played, some of them always got in trouble for running through the sheets of someone's laundry drying on the clotheslines. Some of the mothers seemed to not care about the welfare of their children and let them fend for themselves. Between each duplex unit was a driveway. Not many of us owned cars so the driveways became private play areas for our children. Some people called the Vamp a red light district, which it may once have been. However, when I moved to the Vamp that reputation no longer existed. I feel like our landlord, Mr. Arthur Collier, Sr., was the godfather of low-income housing. My first monthly rent was $25.00 per month. Despite what the Vamp was called, it became home for my two children and me. I had to get a different ride to work because I had been paying and driving for my mother, who would not come to the Vamp. My mother said it was out of her way and she did not like the Vamp because it was for poor people.

The negative definition of the word Vamp may have had a lot to do with why people thought it was a bad part of town. By the World Book dictionary, Vamp means, *an unscrupulous flirt; adventuress;* as a verb it means *to allure or attract a man for the purpose of extortion.* I guess that definition is why my mother thought I moved to a red light district. I knew the Vamp's definition had nothing to do with me nor my character. Once I had a red light bulb in my living room lamp and my mother got needlessly angry with me about the red light bulb. I did not know what she thought the red light meant. She finally told me that it meant that my home was open to attract men for sex and money. Immediately, I removed the red bulb from my lamp. To me, innocently, it was just pretty.

Mr. Ursey Thompson let me join his riders to and from work. On paydays he took his wife and me to buy groceries at Spot Cash grocery store. On Fridays he took us to the laundromat. God was not mad at me, after all, he kept placing people in my presence that helped me meet the needs of my little family.

I set up housekeeping and I bravely faced single life as it really was—*hard.* My mother visited us and said, "You look like you are a little girl, playing house. Can Boonie come to see you?" I told her, "My house is our home and I am not playing." I also told her that my brother could not visit my home. She grew very angry because I did not want him in my home. I did not yield. I did everything I knew to make my little children happy in our new home, a small shotgun apartment. As a young mother, sometimes I knew more of what not to do, based on my troubles with my own mother. My school friend, Ruby

Dee, kept my little children, and her husband approved of our arrangement. Our apartments had adjoining walls and I knocked on her door when I left for work. She listened for my babies to wake up and kept them in our apartment.

Living life as a single mother in my own apartment began to take shape. After setting up housekeeping I began to have more male company than I could imagine. I also learned that many were simply wanting to take advantage of my being single and no longer living in the home of my mother. Those who knew me when I lived with my mother knew they could not bring their ill intentions to her home. I learned how to not allow such men to take advantage of my living single in my home, and I learned *fast.* Often it was rough trying to persuade overbearing men to leave. It was an awful feeling not being strong enough to beat the hell out of some and run them away without waking my children nor disturbing my neighbors. I could not awake my children and cause fear in them for their defenseless mother. Neither could I afford to wake my neighbors because they would surely not believe my innocence and they would subject me to charges of being a "floozy." I developed an attitude that all men were no good.

5

All Men Are No Good

I became very bitter toward men. I felt that they were deceptive and that none were deserving of me. I knew I was not a bad girl. I was being pursued by some of the most handsome and gorgeous men I knew. Yet, I felt none of them would be honest nor kind to me. I knew how to sew very well and I made me a lot of pretty and appealing clothing. Daily, I wore Prince Matchabelli perfume. One night I was wearing Prince Matchabelli and a young man said, ". . . My God! What are you are wearing? It must be some 'Find Me In The Dark.' " We all laughed. Since I cannot smell, his compliment meant that I could wear Prince Matchabelli and know I smelled good.

I met and was pursued by several fine men or hunks, whom many other women wanted, but I played the field. I felt like getting revenge for the way my children's fathers had shattered my life.

I met SSG Ultimate Perry. He had all of the best qualities rolled into one man. He was very good-looking, wore fine clothes; was intelligent, friendly, could dance, was a good conversationalist—and he liked me! He loved to sing the Temptations' song "My Girl" to me as if it had been written by him for me only. He was awesome! I almost let him blow my game of revenge. I loved the idea that I had played and ditched that "fine thing."

Next I met SFC New Buick, who had a reputation of finding pretty women, using them and leaving them. I thought, *he'll be a good challenge for me to find, use and leave, too.* I did. He was super fine and drove a new Buick Electra 225 each year. He dressed well and many pretty women pursued him.

One night, my friend Helen had a house party. I made her a bet that I could call SFC New Buick and get him to quit whatever he was doing and come to her party, simply because I said so. She bet I could not. I used her telephone and called him. About one hour after my call, SFC New Buick drove up. Helen was surprised and we laughed for days. We laughed because I was the victor. We agreed, "If he thinks he is good, ha ha, he's just been had." Soon, I learned all my revenge games and tactics were wrong. The awful thing about revenge is you never get to hurt the deserving ones. The innocent ones thereafter get hurt. Maybe the guilty ones will be hurt by someone else? My heart had little to no room for more pain.

In retrospect, God surely was not pleased with my quest for revenge. But I was not thinking about what if God is getting mad at me. Despite my malicious tactics, God protected me from harm and He did keep me within the arch of His safety. He knew I was worth saving. Thank you, God.

From my point of view, as I began to put things in the right perspective my life seemed not too extremely difficult. I still hungered for better living conditions for my children and me. We moved into a small house two doors from my mother. An awful mistake. About one year later I had to beg my mother to please leave me alone.

6

Nightmares in the Daytime

Ruby Please Leave Me Alone and Don't Take My Baby

I desperately wanted a two bedroom house with a bathtub. I moved to 519 South 17th Street, a house on the corner from 511 South 17th Street, the same home that the Hodge and Burgess families lived in when I was a child. I wanted my children to enjoy living in a house with a private yard in which to play instead of an apartment. I wanted them to have a separate bedroom from me. In our shotgun apartment I slept in the living room on a sofa, and shared the one bedroom furnished for my children.

My mother continued to create confusion in my life. One day she came to my home to badger me. She held a stick in her hand and waved it at me. I begged her to please leave me alone. Soon, she created an awful argument and I asked her to leave my home, but she continued to talk ugly and threatening to me and refused to leave. I grew angrier because I knew she was intentionally disrespecting me in my own home and in the presence of my two children. She waved the stick higher at me as if she was hitting me. I thought she had indeed struck me and I grabbed the stick; then she lunged forward and attacked me.

In self-defense we struggled and I bit her in the eye. Self-preservation is the first law of nature. Immediately I regretted having bitten her, but I had no other defense mechanism. Out of anger, she picked up my baby girl, Charmin LaTrell and ran out of my house. I screamed and cried "Don't take my baby, give me my baby!"

From my point of view, though she was my mother she did not have the right to abuse me. The Bible speaks of not provoking thy children to wrath, but she resorted to the worst form of abuse, taking my little girl from me and ignoring that I screamed and cried defenselessly, "Ruby, please give me my baby!" She would not give me my baby and she laughed at my defenselessness.

Ruby, Please Give Me My Baby

My mother shouted obscenities at me, wiped blood from her eye and ran with my baby into her house at 511 South 17th Street. I followed but she locked me outside. I sat on the porch crying for my baby. Through the screened window, I asked my grandmother, Lillie, "Please let me inside!" Wearily, she said she could not let me in because my mother was her only means of support. Lillie talked to my mother, telling her she was wrong for taking my baby. To resolve the matter, I yielded my baby girl to my mother. My mother only wanted her for an income tax exemption. At the end of the year, my mother asked and I gave her a letter which authorized her to take my baby as her income tax exemption. The absence of LaTrell living with Brian and me made me very sad. Many times I cried for my little girl. I longed for the many pretty things that I knew little girls bring to a family. When I took Brian to visit LaTrell, my mother hid her from us. Brian was too young to understand why his sister did not live with us and he could not understand why his grandmother seemed angry when we visited. I did not know how to solve the problem so I continued to yield to my mother's selfishness.

From my point of view it is wrong for grandparents to create problems between parents and their children. Grandparents' special role should never conflict with that of a child's parent. Grandparents have no right to create havoc in their children's lives nor in their family.

My landlady lived at 517 South 17th Street, between my mother and me. She decided to sell the house but made no mention of it to me. One afternoon, I was awakened from a nap by two white men walking around in my house. I was terribly angry and asked why were they in my house. They explained that they were considering buying the house and that my landlady had given them the authority to look inside. That destroyed my trust in my landlady's respect for me as a renter. It was worsened when I considered that she had known me all of my life and never considered that I might have wanted to purchase the house. I lost all respect for her, too.

A few days later, although I loved having two bedrooms and a bathtub, I moved back to the Vamp because God had foreseen my problems and knew I needed to be out of my mother's reach and wrath. The Vamp apartments still only had one bedroom, a living room, kitchen and showers with a commode and no sink. I also did not like living with so many neighbors who chose not to work. Many of my neighbors played cards all day and partied all night. I also detested their borrowing "stuff" that I worked to buy. Some of them called me "Square Broad."

Many things in my life seemed to still be broken. I thought continuously, *how can I fix any or some of my many broken pieces?* Small things I fixed and larger things I pondered over, daily.

From my point of view, I had to get a better paying job. Civilian Personnel of Fort Hood was not considering my previously attained college studies. My mind had not entertained the fact that the 1954 Civil Rights Act had only addressed school desegregation. I was not thinking about the "Jim Crow laws" and that society felt it did not have a reason to respect fairness toward Negroes. I was naive enough to think that just because I had some education beyond Dunbar High School and was smart, I would be equally and amply rewarded. Not so. I finally had a blazing idea. I wanted to attend Keypunch School.

7

Keypunch Education to Cross the Bridge

I hungered for a better job. While ironing the soldiers' fatigue jackets I found some keypunched cards in the their pockets. I knew how to type and I thought there must be some keypunch positions at Fort Hood for which I would qualify.

I was told by a Civilian Personnel Office representative that I needed more education to get a promotion at Fort Hood. Therefore, I asked my first line supervisor, my only African American supervisor in my thirty-six years of service, to grant me leave to go to Keypunch school, in order to cross the bridge from the laundry into a career path. She laughed at me. She escorted me to the second level supervisor. They laughed at me too and escorted me to the laundry foreman. The laundry foreman, however, saw their laughter as disgusting. He knew they were making mockery of my request for annual leave to gain more education and an opportunity for promotions. He grimaced at them and took my time and attendance card and granted me the required annual leave.

I commuted to International Tabulation Institute in Houston, Texas, via Greyhound bus weekly. In 1962, no school closer to Temple would accept me because of my race. I carried Brian with me each Thursday night. We spent the weekend with Unk's daughter, Cleo Thornton, and her family. I went to class on Friday and Monday mornings.

Once during this time, a travelling L. B. Price man was selling fabric and miscellaneous articles on credit, from his car, in our Vamp neighborhood. As I looked at his merchandise, Brian peeked into the man's car and said, "Uumm, Momma, his car smells like a Greyhound bus." He had traveled with me to Houston so many times on a Greyhound bus, he thought the cool breeze of the air conditioner was like the Greyhound bus. My cousin Cleo's family took care of Brian while I was in keypunch school. With a lot of help and God's guidance, I finished the nine-month course in seven weeks with 1,000 strokes above requirement! More than two years later I was promoted to a GS-02. That promotion was a true twist of fate and resulted in a series of promotions. By that time, of course, I had Garland.

From my point of view, each time I tried to help myself, God helped me, too. I was beginning to learn how to survive in the white man's career field. My heart was still callused against black men and I was pleased to love and then drop the best of men who pursued me. I felt that love no longer mattered because too often I had so painfully loved and lost. There were enough fine young men at Fort Hood to convince me that love had nothing to do with anything that I needed at that time. But, to my heart's surprise, love had everything to do with anything that is important in any real relationship.

8

Love Had Everything to Do With It

I met a marvelous young man who quietly and nonaggressively entered my life without me realizing how close he was getting. He was tall and very good-looking, but he did not seem to realize he was "a real hunk." I could not hurt him at all. He was soft spoken and kind, angelic and so unobtrusive in his total being that I could never imagine him arguing about anything. He was so serene, humble and caring, in fact, that he reminded me of a missionary; so caring that he hitchhiked to Austin, Texas, to take some borrowed money to get a friend out of jail. He knew his friend would be in trouble with the Army if he missed the Monday morning company formation, but he also knew his friend's wife was pregnant and that she needed him at home.

When he voluntarily stepped in and helped his friend, I knew this man did not deserve to be hurt nor played with, at all. His kind of man is rare and very hard to find. After a brief courtship I knew he loved me and we definitely became serious. Still, I felt a little awkward to be loved by such a wonderful and handsome man. After all, I had been subjected to those who hurt me as if it was open hunting season on women all year around. I was still suffering from the "ugly duckling" syndrome and was apprehensive about this truly handsome and wonderful man actually being in love with me. Later, I learned he was married.

His being married crushed me because I held a deep seated feeling against dating married men. When I was four years old, I thought I was in love with a married man named Blackie. Blackie chose his wife over me, at that tender age I vowed to not love a married man. As amusing as the situation was back then, it certainly wasn't this time around. When I confronted my wonderful lover about being married, he humbly said, "I wanted to tell you before but I did not want to lose you." I told him that I held deep values and so much respect for marriage that when I learned Mr. Right Soldier was unfaithful to me, I swore I would never disturb a family. He was hurt, and I terminated our relationship. He told me that he and his wife had separated because when he went into the Army, she had found a new lover.

I never told him I was pregnant. I felt if he knew I was pregnant, the situation would become more complicated. I believe, if he knew I was pregnant, he would have responded differently. I was truly in a predicament which I could not figure out nor did I know how to resolve. Some of the vicious women in the laundry called my pregnancy awful and disgraceful. The laundry gossip reeked with shame on me. People with no reason to be unkind to me seemed to think that humiliating me and my unborn was perfectly okay. Despite what people and my mother said to me, or about me, I could not live with the knowledge of wrecking a marriage. I still will not date married men.

During that time, I learned life is much like card games; sometimes you are dealt a good hand, and sometimes a bad hand. Either way, you have to skillfully play the cards that you are dealt. With a good or bad hand you will lose some and win some. The opponents' skills and strategies have a lot to do with winning and losing. All players must play the hands they are dealt and live with the consequences of a win or loss. With my third pregnancy, I played my hand with the best wisdom and knowledge I had at the time. From my point of view, where else could I go and what else could I do?

I sought God's help again. He did not fail me. I had a healthy pregnancy which told me that God was not mad at me and that He favored my respect for marriage. My third pregnancy was lonelier than the first two, because my heart told me that this marvelous man truly loved me and that my loneliness was self-imposed. I had no one to comfort me, but Brian. Though he was only a baby two and a half years of age, he always said the profound words of wisdom that brought joy to my heart. God equipped Brian to soothe my wounds. I was lonely for my daughter and resented my mother's keeping her from me.

When I first learned I was pregnant I searched for solutions. I thought about abortion, but I could not do that to my unborn. I believed my lover really loved me and I thought if I had his baby, the baby would love me as much as his father had loved me. I was searching for love and I had no clue of where to find it. Also, as I believed my lover loved me, I knew that I could really enjoy loving his child. I was right, our baby has been a source of ever-present love for me all of his life.

Today, thirty-five years later, I still feel bad about my lover's not knowing I was pregnant with his child. I still feel bad, too, about not knowing exactly what I should have done. I do know abortion was not an option. Regretfully, I denied my baby the right to know his father and his father's right to know our son, Garland. It is an albatross I have to bear. I made inquiries about my lover. A friend said he attempted suicide over our separation and was discharged from the Army as undesirable. Another friend said he was a casualty in the war of Vietnam. I don't know the truth. I must live with the pain I have caused both he and our son. It has been painful for me because I will never learn if my decision was good or bad. I do know that life goes on and that is a debt I still don't know how to pay.

9

My Baby's Words Freed Me

My pregnancy was another unhappy state of life. However, I demanded that I would be happy anyway. I made myself plenty of pretty maternity clothes. I kept my hair, skin, and hygiene in top condition. I visited Dr. Bruce for regular checkups. I controlled my food intake and gaining of weight. Though it was hard, I refused to let anyone make me angry. I had learned that the mental well-being and state of mind of an expecting mother has a direct impact on the well-being and state of mind of the child. I stayed positive, happy, healthy, and spiritually intact. My baby was born with all of those valuable traits.

One day in the parking lot of Spot Cash Grocery, a nefarious male neighbor stopped Brian and me, to talk. He talked ugly to me about being pregnant. He cast so much shame on my being pregnant that I terribly wanted to curse. Brian looked up at the neighbor and me. Then Brian said, "C'mon, Momma, you don't have to listen to him." The neighbor and I looked at this little boy of about two and a half years old. The neighbor said to Brian, "Children are to be seen, not heard." I told him, "NO! He is right. I don't have to listen to you." I closed our conversation by walking to the car and leaving the man in the parking lot, standing alone and looking aloof and surprised. I learned from the mouth of my baby that I don't have to listen to anyone belittling me or saying anything offensive to or about me. Brian was defending me and bonding with his brother before Garland was born. I was proud of Brian's wisdom and strength to stand in the gap between me and my spiteful neighbor.

Despite what people said to me or about me, I could not have lived with the idea of having wrecked a marriage. As life is like a card game, I played the hand I was dealt and I won my precious baby Garland. I still don't think God was mad at me. Brian's wise words taught me that a child can be a bigger man than small-minded men who stand in judgment of others. Brian, while just a little boy of two and a half years of age, freed me from ever allowing others to hurt my feelings. He also gave me the right to know that I can walk away and ignore anyone I please, especially those who seek to hurt or destroy my feelings. Thanks to God for giving me such a wise little boy with a message directly from You.

10

Garland's Birthday

On Friday, June 7, 1963, I went to Dr. Bruce's clinic for checkup. Dr. Bruce and I again argued about my delivery date. I wanted Garland to be born on Wednesday June 12th. Dr. Bruce predicted my delivery date would be after the Fourth of July. I insisted that I was ready for delivery much sooner. He yielded and gave me a prenatal examination.

During the examination, he told me, with amazement, "Myrtle, if you can hold this baby until Wednesday, I will induce your labor." I was happy. He reminded me that I had asked him to order a boy when I had Brian. He wanted to know if I wanted a boy or girl. I told him, "Brian has already told me he wants a baby brother, so I have already made Brian a baby brother." I whistled with my labor pains and had an easy delivery. Dr. Bruce and his nurse laughed. Dr. Bruce is now deceased. However, recently Dr. Bruce's nurse saw me in a supermarket. She recalled the time when Dr. Bruce asked if I wanted my boys circumcised. She laughed and said I had told Dr. Bruce, "Yes, he may need that thing someday." I don't remember the incident, but it does sound like one of my little witty quirks of humor. She and I laughed together. She marveled over their ages and our family successes.

From their mother's point of view, I had to make

sound decisions for them the very minute they were born. I thought circumcision would be less painful as babies than when they grew older. I had no sphere of reference for that decision. I had been told that it pained less to be circumcised at birth. Again, God stepped in and helped me to make a wise judgment about something of which I had no knowledge.

After my prenatal examination, I went home and made preparations for delivering my baby the following Wednesday. On Wednesday, June 12, 1963, Garland made his debut in the world. The one thing good that my mother did for me was to bring Gail President to my apartment to help me to prepare for Garland's birth. She also took us to and from the clinic for his birth. As I labored, I whistled and whistled, and then I screamed, "He is coming." Dr. Bruce and staff ran to my bedside. He said, "Myrtle, you have another boy." Everyone cheered and was elated. All I wanted had come to fruition. Dr. Bruce recalled that Brian's little body was covered with white residue of the Argo starch, which I ate excessively. He looked at Garland and asked, "Myrtle, he is covered with red, what is this?" I explained that I ate everything with tomato and Bar-b-cue seasoning, daily. Garland had a red bean shell in his hair. It was funny and we all laughed. God was not mad at me.

Garland was extra healthy, about twenty-three and a half inches tall, weighing almost eight pounds. They cleaned him up and handed him to Gail President. I looked at Gail and sulked. Then we both smiled. We have always teased about my resenting her holding him first. Gail was happy to be there for us and to carry him home. Daily, my mother brought Gail to our home in the Vamp. Gail took extra good care of us. On the second day home, I had an attack of postpartum depression. I cried about everything and nothing. All of my circumstances were far more overwhelming than I could understand. I cried without knowing why I was crying. My eyeballs virtually floated in tears. I pushed my inner organs against my pelvis as if I were repeating his birth. My fragile inner organs protruded outside my body. I cried so hard and long. I frightened Gail.

I had her call Dr. Bruce because I could not stop crying. She explained my condition to Dr. Bruce. He came to my bedside, in the Vamp. He held and consoled me. He explained that postpartum depression happens when women have doubts or insecurities about their birthing experience. He told me I would be able to love this little boy as I loved my first two children. He told me not to worry about providing for him and assured me I could do and be all my baby and I needed. He held me tightly and comforted me in my dire need for support.

Some people were surprised that Dr. Bruce had come to the Vamp. I was not surprised that he came, I always thought he cared more for his patients than the part of town in which they lived. I felt neither my race nor status in life meant anything negative to Dr. Bruce. He was my earthly pillar in a serious time of need. Finally, he calmed me and I was mentally in control and thinking about my role as a parent to my new son. I was grateful for Dr. Bruce's patience and ability to strengthen my fragile spirits. I know that parenting is the one thing I do best. However, Postnatal Syndrome was hard for me, and Dr. Bruce helped me to regain my mental stamina to confront and master another serious challenge in my life, taking care of another little bundle of love. I don't think a general practitioner from Scott & White Hospital would have been equally as sensitive and compassionate about my Postnatal Syndrome as was Dr. Bruce. He was my guardian angel at the time when I needed one most. Thanks, God for my guardian angel, Dr. William J. Bruce.

From their mother's point of view, I did the right thing by having Garland and raising him the best I could. God gave me the wisdom to cherish each day that He has given me to take care of my three children. Garland's birth also brought some pain and agony that I was not expecting, but God gave me the strength to endure.

Again, from their mother's point of view, only the act of sex may be illegitimate, not the resulting precious baby. My baby was a new angel whom I was blessed to have in my camp. In retrospect, each of their births were blessings from God. God gave me more wisdom, more knowledge, more love, and more resources to provide for each of them. With LaTrell, I was without a job and I got my first real job. With both of my sons, I earned greater promotions.

God was never mad at me. He was busy helping me to work and provide the important things for our lives. God never promised that all of my life would be a bed of thornless roses. God knew that I knew roses have thorns, sweet fragrances, and require a lot of work and pruning. He showed me how to nurture my little flower garden. My life, though improving, was becoming increasingly more demanding, and my mother's torment took on many different issues and caused my heart to harden toward her and her actions.

11

Life's More Demanding and So Is My Mother

Now, I had three small children. Each one represented some hard times in my life. However, each of their births represent the best three days of my life. Having three beautiful babies did not cause me to seek any further revenge. It told me to hold on to God's unchanging hands and try to make the best life I could for all four of us. As I looked at them in their beds asleep with no need to fear the next day, I knew God was not mad at me. He was pleased with my efforts and amply rewarded us in all of our needs. He supplied me with adequate wisdom to make wise decisions as it affected both my children and my well-being.

I now had a pretty little daughter and two precious little sons to love and for them to love me, in return. Our new baby-sitter quarreled because I held them so much when I came home from work. She knew that I had no time to pet them through the day because I had to work. I had to catch up petting and loving them at night. I loved rocking them and looking into and rubbing their little faces. I loved bathing and oiling their skin, grooming their hair, and playing goo-goo eyes with each of them. I loved bouncing each of them on my knees and playing peek-a-boo and slapping hands. I loved playing with and kissing their little toes. Fondly, I remember flexing their little toes as I sweetly sang,

This little piggy went to market,
This little piggy stayed at home,
This little piggy had roast beef,
This little piggy had none,
This little piggy cried, me, me, me all the way home.

—Mother Goose

I played toes with them as they grew large enough to know that I tickled the bottom of their feet when I sang "me, me, all the way home." They are grown now, but if I see they're barefoot, I will play with their toes and when I tickle the bottoms of their feet, they laugh just like they did as children. As they grew a little older, we slapped our hands and played, Pitty Pat:

Pitty pat, Pitty pat.
Bake us a man,
Pitty pat, Pitty pat
Roll him, roll him and
Throw him in a pan.

—Mother Goose

After we sang ". . . throw him in a pan," we rolled our hands over each other and pretended that we threw him in the pan and happily laughed, loudly.

From their mother's point of view, I love being their mother, despite the circumstances under which they were conceived. They were precious gifts from God. God also gave me the strength to ignore the vile and unkind ignorance of mankind. Still, God was not mad at me nor my little "Flakes" children.

My Mother's Anger over "Flakes"

One of the worst hurdles for me to jump was my mother's being very angry because I gave my children my father's last name, "FLAKES." I could not understand why she raised that for argument. With hostility and anger, my mother declared I had no right to give her husband's name to some other man's child. She also asked, "Who told you I wanted to be a grandmother, anyway?" I no longer cared what she thought. My heart was turning to stone toward her based on her treatment of me. In a very nasty tone and with a curl in my lip and eyebrow, I told her, "When I got pregnant, I did not have you on my mind at the time." That made her angry. I continued, "My daddy gave me his name and I can do whatever the h— I want with it." She became infuriated. I had learned to totally ignore her torment. I knew she was intentionally hurting me and she enjoyed seeing me unhappy. I never knew then nor did I learn why she joined the vultures who stalked my life with ridicule, hate, embarrassment, discontent, and pain. Today, I still do not understand nor care why my mother tormented me, until her death. I know it is a fact that her torment was deliberate.

From my point of view, my little Brian's wise little words of years before had freed me. Many times I have thanked God for the wise words that dripped from the lips of my little Brian, as he defended me and my character. The freedom I gained from his wise words made me no longer care what my mother or anyone else did or said about me. Today, I still do not listen to anyone who tries to hurt me. God was not mad at me. He was proud of Brian for standing in the gap for Him and freeing me. Mamie Eisenhower once said, "No one can hurt me without my permission." I agree. Today, I do not allow anyone to hurt me and I mean no one.

At this stage of life, I had grown and became more mature in my role as a mother. My little children were growing, seemingly so fast, and it was time for LaTrell to go to school. I had many decisions to make about her education that would impact on the rest of her life. I gritted my teeth and made some hard decisions about confronting my mother, again. It was time for LaTrell to go to school, and I could not allow bad decisions to impact upon her education.

12

LaTrell Goes to School and Brian Stands in the Gap

When it was time for LaTrell to go to public school, I visited my mother and told her, "LaTrell has to come home." My mother was terribly defiant. She did not like losing my little girl as an income tax exemption. My mother's one question was, "Who will take LaTrell as an income tax exemption this year?" My mother was content when I gave her another letter of authority to claim my baby as her income tax exemption. I offered that my mother keep everything that she had bought LaTrell and said, "I will take her home in a towel."

The day I went to her house and to bring LaTrell home, I took a towel with me. I was prepared in case my mother would keep what she had bought my baby. I am sure when I arrived at my mother's home, my presence and demeanor clearly signaled that I was serious and did not plan to accept anything other than to take my baby home. My mother had all of the things she had bought boxed and ready to go with us. She did not confront me as I carried LaTrell to a waiting car. I was no longer bothered or frightened by my mother's evil and hateful ways. I was ready for any problems that she may have created. It was a good and warm feeling to hold my baby and know that she was going home to join our family.

LaTrell was welcomed home by her brothers and the neighborhood children who had enjoyed playing with her when they were smaller. Her coming home renewed our wholesome bonding as a whole family. God was pleased with me and He blessed us, daily. I got help to send LaTrell to school and care for my boys. Her school was diagonally across the street from where we lived and had no major traffic route for her to cross. I groomed her hair at night and fed them breakfast each morning before I left for work. I frequently worked overtime and paid to have her pretty little school dresses ironed. I did a great job of taking care of my children, and God rewarded me with more blessings.

From their mother's point of view, I did everything that I thought God required of me. I provided them good health care and kept them a safe and clean place of residence. I nurtured their emotional and intellectual needs, and I protected them from many of the evils of life. I carried them to church, when we could get a ride. I also sent them on the church bus when we did not have transportation. I was kind and loving to each of them. I know God was not mad at me because He gave us many happy days. He kept blessing me, and my life began to take shape again.

My Life Takes Shape Again with Brian in the Gap

My world began to take shape again. I renewed my self-confidence, and my self-esteem began to reach new heights. Brian called Garland "my baby" all the time.

Brian sensed I needed help and would tell me to change Garland's diaper. Brian did not know that I have no sense of smell, and he was actually helping to keep Garland clean and free from chafing. God can and will fix anything. He gave me a son who could smell for me. Brian was very protective over and proud of Garland. He closely watched anyone who held "his baby."

Brian helped me to feed and give Garland his bottle; he played with and entertained him for hours. He watched and helped me groom him. When Garland could sit alone, Brian began to help bathe him. Once Brian cried because he could not get some dirt off Garland's arms. He called me crying and I explained that what he saw were Garland's veins. He was happy with my explanation because he wanted to get him clean. When Garland was very young and people wanted to look at him in his blanket, Brian stood guard over him and protected him from being touched by others. I approved of his protection because I never wanted dirty hands, smoke, or other germs on any of my babies. I never allowed anyone to kiss my small babies. Germs are hazardous to anyone's health. Brian was acting for me. Everyone could tell that he loved, cared for, and protected his little brother.

From their mother's point of view, Brian evoked pride accepting our baby without being jealous of his being the baby. Jealously never existed between any of my three children for any reason. I regretted having to depend on baby-sitters from my neighborhood because some of them were not as dependable as I felt my children deserved. However, I had to live with changing baby-sitters rather frequently in order to get good care for my children. I had an assurance in that Brian was now big enough to know right from wrong, and he would inform me of the care being provided for Garland and himself.

Regardless of the circumstances, he took care of his brother.

Role Identification

I began to call Brian, "Momma's little man of the house." Immediately he learned to like being the man of the house and did a good job of carrying out his role. His childish wisdom told him that he could take care of everyone and everything. To that end he developed a leadership mentality and an assertive attitude regarding all of our family needs. As the little man of the house, he did things that the man would do. He said "Yes" and "No" when I was not at home, and LaTrell and Garland respected his judgment. He also sat in the chair at the head of the dinner table. I taught them what the head of the table represented, and he felt very special to have the seat at the head of the table. Still, the chair at the head of the table has very special significance in our family.

Brian Takes Care of Garland in a Tornado

When Brian was about three years and eight months, a bad tornado swept through Temple and destroyed many things in our neighborhood. The meteorologist at Fort Hood said the tornado was devastating our neighborhood and cautioned people to not travel if possible.

We listened to the radio as we drove home. It was agonizing and I was in tears. I was visualizing our fragile little apartment not withstanding such a turbulent storm. My worst of imaginings raced before my eyes, total destruction and death. I cried for fear of my children's safety. When I frantically arrived and found them safely tucked away in our home, the frail little shotgun apartment, I praised God. When I twisted the door knob, Brian rushed to me with a hug. He tugged me by my hand to the bedroom and showed me that Garland was safe. He said, "Momma, all those grown folks were running around in the weather hollering. I put my baby and his bottle on this pillow and I sat right here besides him. He drank his milk and went to sleep and I just sat here."

By all standards, he had placed Garland in the safest place of our apartment, in a corner between a tall and heavy chest of drawers and a double dresser. My heart felt a hard jerk. Again I knew God had blessed my little boy with the childish wisdom needed for them to survive that horrible storm. The tornado was so powerful that it ripped the front porch roof off our apartment and tossed it into the back yard in one piece. It was phenomenal because the roof had actually cleared the electrical wires above the duplex shotgun apartments. If the roof had hit the electrical wires, it could have set all our apartments on fire. We were immensely blessed. Their surviving the storm reminded me of the reality that my children were not only blessings from God, but that He also protects them from many different storms of life.

From their mother's point of view, God watches and cares for His own, especially our children when we are not around. I made a serious commitment to God. I would do all that I could to take care of our three children. I have kept my promise. I am convinced all my good fortunes have happened because I was and am a good mother. I am still good to my adult children. People were lying to me, God was never mad at me. The Holy Bible confirms that God said, "I have come so that you may have life and have it more abundantly." My family and I are physical evidence of His meaning more abundantly.

Brian Soothes My Pain

One day, I was racking with emotional pain. I sat on the side of Brian and Garland's bed with my forehead in my hands. Garland was playing on the floor with his toys. Brian was about four years old. He bent over and looked under my hands to see my face and said, "Momma, it can't be that bad." I quickly took control of my emotions and said, "You are right, baby, and you'll never see that face again." Contrary to my beliefs, many years later that face did reappear. When I felt helpless and lonely, God, through Brian, always stepped in and did what only He could do, soothe my wounds and mend my broken heart. God's mercy and grace oozed from that precious little boy into me. God's blessings are continual.

From their mother's point of view, children should not be saddled with the problems of their parents. Especially if it may cause them to feel responsible for their parents' problems. Parents are supposed to fight battles and carry loads, though the loads can get very tough and seem unbearably heavy. God will help carry our loads and lead us when we are in need of right directions. All we have to do is ask and trust in His deliverance and know that His son Jesus will see us through.

From their mother's point of view, the loads, burdens, and problems were mine, because I am their mother. Parents are God's vessels of care for children. Though I often felt alone and abandoned, He saw me through and provided bonding between my children.

Brian and Garland's Bonding Takes Place

My little children became so close that I marveled over their peaceful togetherness. When LaTrell was in school, the boys had a lot of time to be alone and enjoy being brothers.

They played together for hours. They shared life without serious argument or fighting. Brian enjoyed teaching Garland to do lots of things. When Garland began to talk, all of us helped to teach him. Garland had a mind of his own. We often told him to say "Good evening, Miss," he would say "Hello, lady." Brian always wondered why Garland would not say what he was teaching him to say. We learned that Garland loved to please Brian. We assumed that Garland wanted Brian to know that he knew more than one way to say the same thing. I had fun watching them become real good friends. From their mother's point of view, their bonding started as early as Brian learned there was a baby to be born. While I was pregnant, he began to anticipate the new baby. It did not take long for Garland to know that Brian was special and deeply love him, in return. They equally love their sister, and she loves each of them. The three of them enjoyed playing with each other.

One Sunday morning I was very tired and fell asleep on the sofa. Brian and Garland played quietly. They went to the kitchen and began to open sodas. I guess they were fascinated by the Big Red bubbles. Together they opened enough sodas to flood a large portion of the floor covering. I had a hard job mopping up all the sticky stuff. They had a good time. I felt like spanking them, but I knew if I had gotten up sooner to check on them, I could have prevented some of it. I scolded them and it never happened again.

From their mother's point of view, it was my duty to

be more watchful over little fellows as small as they were at the time. It might have sent a stronger signal to them if I had spanked them, but teaching them that it was wrong must have been enough. They never did it again. Corporal punishment has its place, but everything that goes wrong does not merit spankings.

Their Bonding Grows Stronger

As they grew older and they did more things together, I began to say "these boys." The term "these boys" sounded good to Brian and Garland because it meant unity. They liked for me to say "Boys, come here." They would sometimes race to see what I wanted. If one knew the other one had done something wrong, they came together slowly. I sensed that one came to support the other one if either needed an alibi. They depended on each other.

From their mother's point of view, I could see strong bonding between them at a very early age. I also enjoyed seeing them defend each other. From their mother's point of view, my joy was knowing my children enjoyed loving each other and being loved by the other two. I knew loving each other was important to their bonding process.

Brian Napped When a Girl Whipped Garland

Once a little girl, about seven, decided to play mommy and used Garland for her baby. Our baby-sitter was not as attentive as she should have been. The girl was playing spanking the baby. She whipped Garland's back with a switch, which seriously welted his skin. Brian was taking a nap. When the neighbors learned what happened, they began to fear the outcome when I came home from work. The girl belonged to a woman known for fighting, cutting, and whipping everybody she met, including policemen. When I came home, Brian told me the whole story. I looked at Garland's welted back, and I felt the pain for him. Garland was about eighteen months of age. Brian and the neighbors told me who did it and I immediately went to the child's mother's apartment. I told my children to stay home. I did not want them to see the possible outcome.

The neighbors were hovering around their door seals, watching. I told the child's mother what had happened, and I expected her to ensure it never happen again. The mother did not create an argument. She asked, "How do you know Brian did not do it?" Her question was easily answered. I told her, "Brian could not have done it because he loves his brother too much to hurt him." I told her, "If Brian had been awake and aware, you would have come to my house because Brian would have done whatever he could to hurt your daughter."

From their mother's point of view, the child who whipped my baby was acting barbarically and so was her mother. I knew many mothers in our neighborhood pitifully beat their children all the time. I was known for not beating my children and that I would confront anyone who hurt them. I confronted the little girl's mother. If she had wanted to fight about it, I was ready to get it on. Fighting was never my choice of problem solving, but I could and would take good care of myself when confronted.

Again, from their mother's point of view, we must defend our children and they must know we will confront whomever does them wrong or harm. I also knew since I worked so far from home, I needed to set the stage for everyone to know I did not take any jive about the safety and well-being of my children.

Finally, from their mother's point of view, it did not bother me that her mother was called bad. It did not bother me that this large and strong lady had whipped two policemen and was charged for destroying their uniforms. I knew the saying, "Let's get it on," and I was prepared to rumble. God was not mad at me. He calmed her nature in favor of what was right. Right meant she would teach her daughter right from wrong and not to whip babies.

Brian Packs Their Clothes, to Leave

Brian and Garland's being three years apart allowed them to enjoy their roles as big and little brother. Brian became more protective over Garland as they grew older. One day Brian was so unhappy with the baby-sitter that he packed some of Garland's and his things, in a brown paper bag, to go and stay with my maternal grandmother, Lillie, who had returned from the Texas State Sanitarium in 1955. The State of Texas had told my mother that she would have to start paying for Lillie's care in the hospital or they would take ownership of Lillie's home to compensate for her stay in the state hospital. My mother took her mother, Lillie, out of the sanitarium and returned her to 511 South Seventeenth Street. My mother did not seek professional care for Lillie's mental state of mind. God blessed Lillie with a desire to not venture away from home. Once, she left the house to buy some cigarettes. When she discovered she was totally lost because the neighborhood had changed so drastically, she found her way home and never left again. She enjoyed my taking her for a ride to show her how Temple had changed during the twenty years she was in the state hospital. Back to my boys, they wanted to stay with Lillie. Lillie was glad to care for my little boys.

From their mother's point of view, I was pleased that Brian could and did tell me our baby-sitter was neglectful and unkind. I was proud that he saw through what others called crazy or mental illness and knew my grandmother, Lillie, loved and could take care of them. God had blessed us with a loving great-grandmother who stood in the gap when she was needed. She was not crazy; she talked to herself and smoked a lot of cigarettes. Many so-called sane people talk to themselves and some argue with their answers. Lillie's smoking was a pastime or habit that most adults possessed. Lillie had a much greater sense of family values and love than did Ruby. Lillie liked having fun in her own special and humorous way. I loved every ounce of her beautiful and kind persona.

Lillie loved keeping Brian and Garland; she knew they were her little great-grandsons. I felt that she loved me for trusting my sons to her care. My car pool allowed me to drop them off in the morning and pick them up in the evening. They became bonded with Lillie. I liked that because they can remember their great-grandmother. Since there were no other children, their bond became stronger with her and each other. Brian entertained Garland while Lillie scrubbed her house and tended her yard. Their summer baby-sitter, Gail President, lived next door. Gail was a teenage daughter of MaeMae, who is the godmother of all three of my children. Gail loved Brian and Garland, and she helped to make their bond stronger. MaeMae saw Brian as her little boy since she kept him from birth. Gail saw Garland as her baby because Dr.

Bruce handed him to her before I held him, a precious memory we hold dear. The President family was always great for my children and me. I shall always remain grateful to them for their love and support in all of my life's rough and good times.

From their mother's point of view, God always provides for those who love Him and keeps His commandments. The Lord knew, I was trying. He made Lillie available when we desperately needed her and He provided the President family for reinforcement. I could not foresee that God had a house in His plans for my family. I only knew that I prayed for another house and better living conditions for my family.

13

A New House and Life in the Vamp

Life continued to treat us better. I continued to pray that we could live in a house instead of my little shotgun apartment. I had liked living in a house as a child; one of the main things I wanted for my children was to have a nice room of their own with no closed doors. Roomers had kept our doors closed, and I gained a phobia about closed doors. There was a little white house across the street from the apartments. I was told that it was going to be available for rent. I pursued getting the little white house before the people moved. Mrs. B. Kay Hornsby, one of my mentors, had taught me, "Good things comes to those who wait, . . . but it is what is left from those who hustle."

I learned to believe in hustling. We moved into the white house directly across the street from my shotgun apartment. The house was pretty, and it sat behind a white picket fence. A white picket fence was another feature that made 511 South 17th Street very special; it also had a picket trellis with a love seat at each end of the double gate leading to the garage. There were many things about 511 South 17th Street that were structurally beautiful, but it was never a real home for me. After moving into the white house, I got a purebred collie puppy and named him Collie. Collie was the name of my little cousin William Oscar Horton's collie dog. Naming my collie Collie gave me a visible piece of my love for William Oscar, whom I affectionately call "my W. O."

I bought plenty of outdoor play equipment for my children—a safe private play area. The children's playmates fondly said we lived in the "white house." Living in the white house was a major accomplishment for me because it had a real living room, a spacious kitchen, two bedrooms, a bathtub, a private yard, and a clothes line behind the house. Having a bathtub was very important for me to provide for my children. I never liked our sinkless shower with a commode and a drain hole in the floor. Later we got a washing machine connection in the house. *WOW!!* What a treat to only have to go to the laundromat to dry clothes when the weather was bad or cold.

I taught each child how to drive our car at age ten. It was for emergency purposes only. However, the neighborhood laundromat was only three and one-half blocks away with virtually no traffic. I let LaTrell drive to the laundromat. Our neighbors could not believe she could drive so safely, so young. Though it was illegal, we took the risk and God blessed her to never have an accident or get a ticket. To date, she has received only one traffic ticket and it was not for a moving violation.

From their mother's point of view, taking good care of children also means providing them with some of the gadgets that make life more comfortable. The washing machine and the car were real blessings.

I Will Hit You with My Cast

The yard toys consisted of a swing set with a ladder and slide, a whirley bird, a see-saw, a set of monkey bars, and several yard games. We enjoyed playing horse shoes and croquet. Marion's grandfather, Daddy Ben, had taught us how to play both games, and I wanted to teach my children how to pitch horse shoes and play croquet. Our yard was as equipped as a city park. The neighborhood children could not resist the temptation of playing in our yard whether we were at home or not. My first rule was that no one was allowed to play in our yard when we were not at home. I felt responsible for anyone who might get hurt. My children respected my rules, especially for no company when I was not at home. Garland's playmate Douglas insisted on breaking our rule "Don't come into our yard when we are not at home." Garland told Douglas to stay out of our yard and to not play with his red wagon when we were not home. Douglas seemed to think our rules were a joke or not applicable to him. He broke all our rules, repeatedly.

While Garland had a cast on his arm, he told Douglas, "If you come in our yard or take my wagon, I am going to hit you on your head with this cast." Douglas must have thought Garland was joking. Later we returned home. Douglas had been in the yard and taken Garland's red wagon to his house. Garland searched until he found Douglas. He hit Douglas on his head several times with his cast and took his wagon. Brian told me, "Garland hit Douglas on his head with his cast." I questioned Garland about hitting Douglas. He calmly told me, "Momma, I told him to stay out our yard and to leave my wagon alone. I told him I would hit him on his head with this cast and I did."

I could tell Garland was serious about Douglas breaking my rule and more so, his rule about his wagon. I asked how did Douglas take Garland's hitting him on his head with the cast. They all laughed and agreed, "Douglas's head was so hard the cast did not hurt." I smiled because it was rather funny. Garland was so serious and angry that he was also funny. When Douglas's mother heard about the incident, she laughed and said, "I bet he'll stay out your yard and leave that wagon alone." Brian was not involved in "the cast whipping story," but he did express the thought that Douglas should have respected Garland's rules about his wagon and playing in our yard when we were not at home. LaTrell felt the same about Garland having a right to hit him on his head. She felt Douglas should have known Garland would hit him as he promised.

From their mother's point of view, they learned very young to respect authority. They also wanted their friends to respect my authority, and they wanted to take good care of the things I provided for their pleasure. Simply stated, they did not want others to destroy what I worked so hard to provide for them. I thought they were to be commended for protecting our property. I did caution Garland to not use his cast as a weapon.

The fenced-in yard and gate gave us privacy and the right to have a dog. Dogs began to serve many purposes in our lives, and our sharing the responsibility of the dogs made family bonding even more important.

14

Dogs, A Frog, and Now a Cat—Family's Best Friends

Collie

Collie knew he was my dog more than the children's, and he missed me while I was at work. He finally picked up his bone and moved to another house where he loved another lady and she loved him. I did everything I knew how to keep him at home. I bought a big heavy screw and staked it in the ground. Collie learned how to entangle his chain and pull the stake out of the ground. I exhausted all ideas of how to keep Collie at home. I visited the lady and apologized for his insistence on staying at her house. She was happy that he came to see her and enjoyed him because she was a homemaker and no one was home with her through the day, but my dog. I finally agreed to let him stay with her, and I visited him at their house. Collie and I hugged and played when I visited their home. They moved to another location and we visited their new residence. When he saw us, he ran and jumped in the car through the open window of my tiny red Falcon. My mother was with us; he lapped, kissed, and walked all over us. We could hardly get out the tiny car for this big loving salivating collie dog. All of us laughed because he was so excited. The family moved to the country, and we lost contact with Collie. I really felt good because the new family took good care of Collie, and he was happy.

From their mother's point of view, though the dog was mine, the children shared in the love and care for our pet, Collie. We hated it when he moved because loving Collie was a real family affair.

Prince, Alias Princess

Prince was a jet black cocker spaniel. We all shared his love. Prince clung to Brian, and he loved Prince as if Prince belonged to him only. As Prince grew, we noticed Prince had too much boy dog company late at night. When Prince started to getting too fat, we learned Prince should have been named Princess. We were tickled when our family friend Sugarman laughed at us and said, "Y'all don't know a girl from a boy." At that point, we changed Prince's name to Princess. Princess was heavy and expecting to deliver puppies anytime soon. Once as I left going to work, my last words were, "Brian, do not let Princess in the house; she is about to have puppies." It was a dark cool and rainy day. Princess clung close to Brian as he was preparing to leave for school. Brian's little heart could not let him lock Princess outside in the cool rain. He let her in the house out of the rain and went to school. They said that Garland reminded Brian of my last words, "Don't let Princess in the house."

Upon their return from school, they found Princess had delivered the puppies in their bed. Brian was very happy about the puppies but afraid because of the messy bed. He took the cover off the bed and made it up with clean linen. He met me at the car full of smiles and told me how many puppies Princess delivered. Garland laughed and said, "She had them in our bed." Brian hurriedly said, "But I cleaned up behind her." I went into the house and looked for signs of afterbirth; there were none. I sighed with relief. As I went to the bathroom, I glimpsed a sheet with blood and afterbirth stains hanging from the dirty clothes hamper.

I screamed for Brian to come to me; all three came. I asked about the sheet in the hamper. All three of them looked speechless. I pulled the cover back on the bed and UGH!!! All three began to explain and Garland laughingly told me the funny things about Brian trying to clean up the afterbirth. They, especially Garland, had learned how to tell stories with flair and fun in order to make the punishment lighter. He has a knack for humor in serious times, and it has always worked. I don't know from whom they got their humor. They declared that I was humorous too. I began to laugh as they told the story of Princess having the puppies in the bed. It was still raining, and I had to get the mattress out of the house. It stunk. I wrestled with the mattress and got it on top of our car. The next day when I tried to take it off our car, it was wet from the rain, it was extra heavy with water, and I was not as strong as I thought. The mattress fell on top of me, and I fell in the mud. Don't you laugh at me. They knew not to call it funny. I was a wet and nasty unhappy camper. They secretly laughed at me and the wet mattress struggle. When I managed to get up from the mud, I was fuming. I cleaned up and drove the car from under the mattress. In the next few days, the mattress dried and the rain had washed it clean. After my anger died, they turned it into a joke and I laughed with them.

From their mother's point of view, boys will be boys and a sick dog gets to the core of a child's heart. The whole

Prince story was funny. We all thought Prince was a boy until he was with puppies, and we changed his name to Princess. Did they get a whipping? No, but we never had another mother dog. LaTrell and Garland defended Brian and were glad that Princess was not in the cool rain.

Again from their mother's point of view, at the onset, none of this was funny, I was too wet, dirty, and tired for humor. In the end, I admired Brian's love for his dog and the puppies. I admired the subtle way in which LaTrell and Garland tried to help Brian and the dog. Brian took care of Princess and her puppies. He helped to get them good homes. Pets help to build character, also. When a child learns to take good care of a pet, it teaches him or her responsibility. Accepting responsibility is lacking in many of youth today.

Nip

Nip followed Princess. Nip was a small dog and followed my children home from downtown. It was the cutest little hairy dog. It was accustomed to living in a house, and I was unaccustomed to any dog being in the house. The children named the dog Nip and kept her in the house, at first without my knowledge. We watched the daily newspaper for lost-dog ads. We knew it had been a favorite pet because she wore a collar and was well disciplined. No one advertised for her return. She never barked in the house. When we left the house, the children laughed after we were several blocks away from home because Nip would get into the car and hide under my seat. When we were a good distance from home, Nip would come from under my seat, play with the children, and look out the back window. The children enjoyed Nip's hid-ing from me and we could tell she was accustomed to riding in the car.

We frequently went to Belton Lake for recreation and to picnic. They allowed Nip to hide and go to the lake. We were surprised, when we stopped at the lake. Nip jumped out of the car and ran straight into the lake. We all screamed, "Nip, Nip, come back." Nip did not listen to us or pay us the least bit of attention. Nip sprung up into the air, jumped into the lake, and swam far into the water. The precious little dog could swim fast and far. Nip always returned and we all hugged our swimming little wet and hairy dog. When Nip shook the water off her body, we laughed and got wet. We believe someone stole Nip. I decided that we would not have another dog. It seemed, soon as we became attached to one, something painful happened and we lost another one.

From their mother's point of view, when necessity warrants changing past practices, it is okay to do so. I thought I would never allow a dog to live in the house. I changed for Nip because she was house broken, small, and well trained. My children learned that with the right conditions, exceptions may be made.

Tramp

Tramp was a strange-looking dog that came from somewhere unknown. He appeared to have adopted us. He had light yellow, piercing eyes and looked serious all the time. He had short black-and-white hair and never let any of us touch him. When we tried to touch or pet him, he ran and hid under the house. When it was hot, his skin appeared to turn red under his short black-and-white hair. He was a strange dog and I named him "Tramp." He seemed to already know my rule of no company and the children's not being allowed to leave home when I was not at home. Tramp would not let my children leave or let other children enter our yard, when I was not at home. When he gritted his teeth and snarled an awful growling sound, my children stayed in our yard and the neighbor's children stayed out. My children learned that Tramp was their protection and made them stay home. He earned his keep and we all loved him, too. I bought Tramp good food and gave him fresh water, daily. He earned his "room and board."

My friend Helen once tried to enter my house when I was not at home. She thought if the screen door was unlocked, she could leave me a note. Tramp barked, snarled, and growled at her, but she kept coming. When she reached for the doorknob, he nipped the bottom of her rear end just enough to let her know he meant business. She was angry at Tramp and never returned. Tramp always followed our car to the corner when we turned left and ran home when we were out of sight.

While we were packing and moving from the Vamp to South Thirty-fourth Street, Tramp followed me to the corner. I turned right instead of left, as he was accustomed to. I hit him and he died instantly. He did not bleed at all; the tires must have crushed his internal organs. I still wonder why he did not bleed. He did not make a sound and none of his organs were exposed. He just died. I had a man put his body in a box, and I took him to the pound for proper disposal. Though he was strange, he deserved proper disposal. He was my best friend and a welcomed baby-sitter. He took good care of my children and our home.

From their mother's point of view, Tramp was an integral part of our family and helped to protect each of us.

Tramp taught us the true meaning of the saying "a dog is man's best friend."

Pierre

Pierre was pure-bred poodle. Though I vowed that we would not have another dog, a man gave us a black poodle and we named him Pierre. Pierre was wild and rowdy. He was playful and energetic. His energy outlasted our energy all the time. We let his hair grow extra long so that people would not know he was a poodle; nevertheless someone stole him. Pierre played with all the neighborhood children. If they threw a ball, Pierre would fetch it and play as long as they wanted to play.

From their mother's point of view, our dogs were an integral part of the children's growing up and they helped my children's bonding process. Our dogs gave my children something to share, to love, and they shared the love that the dogs gave in return. Our dogs gave them a boost when their chips were down. When they helped to care for our dogs, they were sharing an experience of responsibility. I never minded them having a dog, but one at a time, because I never liked multiple pets. I never liked pets in the house. Yet, Nip stole my heart and was an exception.

Brother Me

Brother Me was a Heinz 57, no one breed over another. My brother gave him to me, so I was really creative and named him "Brother Me." Our friends always laughed at his name. He was the last dog we owned because the children were entering adulthood and did not have time to help me take good care of him. Once I went to a meeting overnight and failed to leave enough food until I returned. He lived in the backyard with no place to hustle food. When I came home and opened the back door, Brother Me savagely raced past me and attacked the refrigerator. I opened the door and let him eat whatever he could find. I let the dog catcher take him to the pound for adoption. I never believed in having a pet and not being able to provide it with good care.

Brian's Frog

Frequently, I cleaned the children's bedroom thoroughly. They did the usual, "go to your room and clean it up" type cleaning. I pulled their bunk beds from the wall. There I found odd socks that had missed many wash days, fruit peelings from fruit they ate in bed, and fell asleep while eating. I found pieces of toys that they thought were lost. I also found a small brown paper bag. The top of the suspicious-looking bag was tightly twisted. I felt a little leery about the puffy paper bag. I squeezed the bag and it puffed out. I squeezed the bag and it puffed out again. After the fourth squeezing and puffing, I cautiously tried to look inside the bag. I carefully opened the little brown bag. As I peeked into the bag, big eyes glared back at me. I jumped and closed it. I tried again and the big eyes glared at me. I jumped and closed it again. Finally, I gained enough courage to explore the bag further. Slowly, I tore the paper away and saw the big glaring eyes belonged to a big fat freshly dead frog.

I called out, "Boys, come here." All three came. I was standing and holding the paper bag. When they saw the paper bag, their eyes were as wide as the frog's eyes. I held the bag out and asked, "Who owns this bag and frog?" They all laughed and began a unified defense for Brian. Garland started a funny story and LaTrell laughed as Brian tried to explain why he put the frog in the bag. Brian said, "One night as you were coming to our room, I hid the frog in the bag. After you left our room, I forgot to let the frog out of the bag and it was smothered to death." I had to laugh with them. They asked me to show them how I responded to the little brown bag when I picked it up and it puffed back at me and how I responded to the big glaring eyes. Very dramatically, I showed them and we all laughed.

From their mother's point of view, they were each other's lawyers and they made a good team. Any one of them could and would bail the other one out of trouble. It was like having three Johnny Cochrans in one house. Isn't that what brothers and sisters are for? Yes, to defend each other when it is not harmful. Whenever all three shared in a problem, it generally ended in laughter. Garland could find something to laugh about no matter what the problem.

Again, from their mother's point of view, the innocence of children causes them to do some of the funniest and dumbest things. If parents recall some of our own childhood pranks, we would admit the cycle does repeat itself.

Miss Sugar, the Cat

Today, I have my first cat, Miss Sugar Captain. She is definitely a house cat, gets off with plenty of cat-type mischief, and sheds her white hair on my navy blue velvet sofa. I must be growing softer with age. From my children's point of view, it is puzzling how I have become attached to a cat. Brian has expressed the feeling that he is glad that I have Miss Sugar because pets are good company and give unconditional love. Miss Sugar stole his heart during his Christmas visit. Miss Sugar crawled on to Brian's chest as he lay asleep in our lounge chair, and she went to sleep, also. Garland has allowed me to bring Miss Sugar with me when I visited his home in Beaumont. LaTrell thinks Miss Sugar is neat and was the first to tell me how clean cats are and how affectionate they are to their owner. How does Miss Sugar fit into their bonding? She is very important and their acceptance of her is bonding extended. They love my having love in my home. Miss Sugar Captain is special, spoiled, and does anything she wants to do and I love it. I hope I am blessed to own her for years to come.

Garland KaZell Flakes, Brian Tenell Flakes, and
Charmin LaTrell Flakes

Family fun: Brian, Myrtle, LaTrell, and Garland.

Brian, Mom, Garland, and LaTrell

Charmin LaTrell's debutante ball: Brian, Mom, Garland, and LaTrell(seated).

Garland's wedding day: Brian, LaTrell, Delena Kay, Garland, Myrtle, and Keith KaZell.

Uncle Brian and Brittany

Warden Garland KaZell Flakes

Brian Tenell Flakes enjoying his job as a truck driver.

15

Cars Are Fun and Necessary

I worked at Fort Hood for nearly eight years and could not afford a car. My small hard-earned money had its priorities. A car was below ten on my list of priorities. In 1965 while a GS-2, I asked my supervisor if she felt any threat to the future of my job. She said, "No." I started shopping for a car that I could afford on a GS-2 salary while providing the basic necessities for my children and me. Our first little car is still a pleasant memory for me. It represented a major milestone of accomplishment in our lives.

Uby, Uby, You Broke Our Car

After getting settled in the white house, I got our first car, a cute little red, two-door 1962 Ford Falcon Futura. It was snazzy. We loved our cute little red car. It had leather bucket seats and standard shift transmission. It only cost $800 and that was what really mattered. I financed it through my Federal Credit Union. Literally, I could not drive it off the dealer's lot. On my first day of trying to drive it, I sat at a red light not knowing how to find first gear. A longtime family friend, O. B. Goodlowe, stopped to help. I was crying and told him I could not make my little car go. He saw that it was standard shift and said, "Well, baby, remember what the man told you and you will make it go," and he left. I would never have guessed that he could not drive a standard shift, either.

Finally, I found the first gear and I went to my mother's house. She was surprised that I had a car and was more surprised that it was standard shift. She could not drive a standard shift either. Brian was riding with me and teasing me because I could not drive the standard shift. He laughed so hard that I left him with my mother. I asked her neighbor to teach me how to find the gears. She did. When she and I returned, Brian was very happy that I could "handle it." He knew I wanted to provide our own transportation. All three children were proud of our little red car. Garland loved to stand behind me, and Brian liked the front seat. LaTrell was easy to please. It was fun to own a car.

From their mother's point of view, the little red car brought many things within our reach and made us happy. For me, it was also transportation to work and running the required errands. For my children it meant going places we could not have walked. It gave us a sense of adventure and pride. Sometimes, I allowed one of my children to take company when we went joy riding. As Garland grew taller, one day after his head bumped the ceiling, he said, "Momma, I think our car is getting liller and liller." I knew that he was growing and that meant we needed a larger car.

One Fourth of July, we were returning from Belton Lake celebrations. I hand-signaled to left turn and my mother, behind me, was not paying attention. She attempted to pass us while I was turning left. She hit our car in the rear and left side. People came from everywhere to witness the mother-and-daughter wreck. The onlookers began to say who was right and who was wrong. I shouted, "All of you shut up. This is my momma and my wreck and is none of your business." They shut up. My mother attempted to make it my fault; it was not. Garland got a nasty bump on his forehead. Garland told her, "(Ruby) Uby, Uby, Uby, you broke our car, look what you did to our pretty 'lil, car, Uby, you done broke our car." I was angry with her because I could not believe she was so careless. LaTrell and Brian were sad too. We got our little red car fixed and we were happy again. From their mother's point of view, children know when progress is being made in a family and should be included in some of the decisions. Participation in family decisions builds character within children and helps them to establish goals for their adult lives.

We Got a Bigger Car

Our second car was a 1965 white Ford Falcon Futura, four-door with an air conditioner. We went to Georgetown to visit my Caucasian friend Johnny Melton. Johnny was medically retired with severe multiple sclerosis. Johnny told me, ". . . Myrtle, next time you come to Georgetown, to see me, just keep going and go to Austin and then keep going to San Antonio and just keep on going." I grasped the picture immediately. I began to think how happy we would be riding across these United States sight-seeing and visiting things and people while sleeping in hotels/motels and eating in fancy restaurants.

Johnny Melton sparked my love for traveling for the rest of my life. Johnny and I shared a special black female and white male friendship, despite society's non-consenting at the time. Johnny also enjoyed making huge rocking horses. He gave my children two. They were large with huge springs in the back, leather ears, braided yarn manes, well-defined eyes, and metal bridles with leather reins. They were so durable that my children enjoyed them for a long time, and I also rode the wooden horses. When they were asked about the play horses, they loved to say "Momma's friend Mr. Melton in Georgetown made them for us."

The Rest Were the Best

A 1970 Chevrolet Impala took us on many vacations that are referred to in the bonding of highway stories. A 1973 burgundy and black Oldsmobile was the envy of Temple High School. It was part of my growing image professionally, socially, and civically. LaTrell frequently drove it to school. All three of my children felt very special because I allowed her to drive our best car to school. The Flakes children were riding in class. Once LaTrell said, "Momma, we have the best-looking car in the black parking lot." I had to have more explanation about the black parking lot. When she explained that Caucasian children parked in one area and black children parked in another, I was amazed. I told her that they were probably the only children with a momma who was fool enough to let such a nice car go to school. We all laughed, but I always taught all three of them that General Motors can make cars faster than I could pay for them, and they never made one that was better than either of them.

A 1974 green Chevrolet Van bonded the total community. Garland's playing basketball became the focus of my attention. I took part of the girls' basketball team to see the boys play out of town. I also took some of the boys to see the girls' basketball team play out of town. Brian and LaTrell thought it was wonderful that I supported Garland and his friends. I also loaned our van to churches and organizations for out-of-town group travel. When I administered the summer employment program at Fort Hood, I transported youth to work. It was truly a community service van. Brian, Garland, and LaTrell were always pleased that our van offered traveling opportunities for other children. They recalled how much they learned from traveling. Regretfully, a lady once used it to take children to Waco to be on television. She threw a rod and left the van on the side of the road. I had it towed home and parked in our back driveway. Much later, a Mariachi band bought it and fixed it for their road van. It still serves the community.

Our cars that followed the van came after all three of my children were young adults. However, each of my children always wanted me to own good, dependable, and pretty cars. Unitedly, they have agreed that from their point of view, I needed and deserved good and pretty cars. They knew I had provided nice cars for their pleasure.

From their mother's point of view, it is good to give children tangible things to make them happy, but to give them intangible things of value such as respecting special friendships will positively impact their lives for the rest of their lives. Each of the cars we owned while they were children were shared with many others of our community. Cars were a lot like our dogs. Each one served a special purpose but were never more important than any one of us as a family member. God was not mad at me. He was busy making good things happen for us and ensuring that we shared safe trips, over thousands of miles.

16

Flagg Brothers Shoes and a Green Leather Coat

Brian loved for Garland to dress like him. He asked for Garland to have some of the same things he wore. Garland wanted whatever Brian wanted for him. Very early, Garland grew taller and heavier than Brian. Sometimes Brian seemed to resent Garland's rapid growth, but he continued to love him more and called him "my baby." When Garland started to school, Brian was in the third grade. Brian let it be known Garland was his little brother. Immediately they were known as the "Flakes Brothers." Such unity made them happy. Sibling unity and love, a joy I never experienced. My brother and I never had the joy of unity. Brian fell in love with and wanted some Flagg Brothers Shoes. I took them to a big mall in Austin, to the Flagg Brothers Shoes store. The salesman said Brian's feet were too small. Garland tried on some and they fit. Brian was disappointed because his feet were too small. Garland told me, "Momma, I want to wait until Brian's feet are big enough for him to wear some, too." I could hardly contain my joy over how much he wanted to make his brother happy. Brian was happy when Garland voluntarily chose to wait until his feet grew larger. Later, we returned to the Austin's Flagg

Brothers Shoes store. Still, Brian's feet were not large enough, but he wanted them so badly that the salesman put cotton in the toes of their smallest pair. On that second trip, they both got a pair of Flagg Brothers Shoes.

From their mother's point of view, it was sweet of Garland to voluntarily choose to wait until Brian's feet grew enough for him to wear some, too. Garland wanted Brian to be happy, and he felt Brian would be happier if they both owned the coveted Flagg Brothers Shoes.

Additionally, from their mother's point of view, if Brian's happiness was so important to Garland that he wanted to wait, I gladly let him. They were happy when Brian got some Flagg Brothers shoes. My allowing Garland to wait embraced their unity and bond.

Leather Jackets and a Green Coat

The Flagg Brothers Shoes made my boys feel very happy and special. Many of their friend's parents would not drive to Austin just for a certain brand of shoes. To me it was no big deal. Austin is only about sixty-seven miles from Temple; it was a nice outing. Brian's being three years older than Garland made him more fashion conscious earlier. Brian also had very good taste in clothing. However, he always wanted Garland to have what he wanted for himself. While out shopping, Brian saw two leather jackets, one black and one wine; he loved those leather jackets. Brian asked if he and Garland could have the beautiful jackets. I wanted them to have some, also. Brian begged and begged for the black jacket and a wine jacket for Garland. I told Brian they were too costly and I could not afford to buy them. He was very sad, but he did not badger nor make me feel guilty for not having the money. I explained to him that we could not afford the price of the jackets. He was sad, yet he appeared to understand.

A few days later, I bought the leather jackets. His was black and Garland's was wine. Brian came home first and saw I had spread the jackets on their bed. Brian's happiness exploded; he literally ran into me with hugs and kisses of thanks. He raced outdoors and called Garland. He eagerly showed him his wine leather jacket. Garland was happy and grateful, too. He was happier because Brian had gotten the jacket he wanted, so badly. Both of them were fancy-looking guys in their Flagg Brothers shoes and leather jackets. Brian said he was so happy that he slept in the jacket. He wanted to rush the next day so he could wear it to school. His friends really liked their jackets, and that made Brian extra proud.

There was a beautiful emerald green leather coat with white shoe lacing in the back and part of the front. I bought it for LaTrell, from our favorite dress shop, LaBonita's. I also bought her some knee-high leather boots. Her shopping at LaBonita's was a treat because mostly women with good jobs shopped at LaBonita's. She like shopping there, and some of her friends wished they did, too. I had three happy and smartly dressed children. She in her knee-high leather boots and emerald-green leather coat and my sons in their Flagg Brother's Shoes and leather jackets. They were looking good, feeling proud and very grateful children. I was happy because they were very happy and looked good. I relished the idea of my children looking good. How well children looked often was a symbol of how much their parents loved them. I also taught them always to look good when I came home from work. They knew I could possibly take them somewhere special and I insisted they be well groomed and presentable. When I came home and they were untidy, I said they looked as if the Boogey Woman was their mother. They hated to have me refer to myself as the Boogey Woman. To call me the Boogey Woman brought tears to their eyes. They would get angry enough at me to cry. Either one or all three would say, "You are no Boogey Woman, and don't say that." I stopped teasing them because they were serious.

From their mother's point of view, they needed a jacket and a coat. It was proper to get the ones they wanted. They needed shoes; it was proper to get the ones they wanted. Driving to Austin to a super mall was a joy ride that made them very happy and grateful. It was during the Christmas holidays, and the Austin mall had enormous decorations that made our trip seem so very special. They got special pleasure from knowing they went out of town to buy something special.

Again, from their mother's point of view, children don't really ask for much and two trips to Austin for the Flagg Brothers shoes was a treat that none of us have forgotten. God was not mad at me, He was proud of me. I know He was proud of me because He kept providing avenues through which I could continue to make my children very happy.

17

A Pit Toilet and Who Did It

My dad's only living sister still lives in Somerville, Texas. She is a remarkably healthy and Christian woman and can whip up a good meal in a matter of minutes. She keeps her freezer full of her fresh garden foods and meat. She is over eighty-six years of age and is the last link to my father's lineage. I have always taught my children to love and respect Aunt Etta because she is their great-grandfather's sister. She is the last of twelve children born to Mack and Edna Flake. I did a good job of teaching my children to honor her, and their love means a lot to her and them. Garland never forgets her birthday and visits her at least three times a year. His children know and respect her as their great-grandfather's sister. She welcomes their visits and affectionately calls Garland, "Sweets."

History in many small towns includes the famous pit toilets. They generally were built quite a distance from the main house. Yet, they were always close enough for women and children to feel safe while in the pit toilet. Some were neatly painted and well constructed and others were not special at all. I saw plenty of one-hole pit toilets and knew owning a two-holer was an image of upper class. I wondered why they built two-holers. I never saw two people go to use it at the same time.

I could not smell. Therefore the odor in the pit toilets never bothered me. As a kid, when Aunt Etta could not find me, she'd recall, "I bet she is looking at a book in the pit toilet." She was right. Many days she scolded me and said, "You are not at home where you flush the commode as you read a book." She also said, "Wipe up and read your book somewhere else." I think Aunt Etta knew I could not smell or surely she wondered how I could stand the odor of a hot summer's pit toilet, while reading a book.

Garland recalls when I took them to visit Aunt Etta, the two-holer pit toilet was still in vogue. I always stopped in town and had them to use the Texaco Service Station rest rooms. I explained to them that the pit toilet was not as sanitary as our bathroom and smelled offensive. They never debated my wise judgment for their well-being, so we used the toilet at the downtown Texaco Service Station.

I did not know that my explanation only heightened their curiosity. While we visited and I was preoccupied in conversation with Aunt Etta, Brian and Garland explored the two-holer pit toilet. Brian, being the older, took the responsibility of being sure Garland did not get too close while peeking into the holes. To have fallen in would have been really bad, whew!! They learned it looked like a small house with a door and a small piece of wood that rotated on a nail from the outside and a hook on the inside. Aunt Etta had a richer one; it had commode seats with lids. The lower back was open. I guess that was the ventilation system and the hole in the ground was very deep, with maggots. Often Aunt Etta put lime and/or sulfur in the bottom of it for sanitizing and to reduce the odor. After Brian and Garland had given the two-holer pit toilet a good look and the odor was overwhelming, they knew why I had them to use the restroom in town. The building never became completely common. Each time we visited, they had to peek into the two-holer pit toilet.

I learned that children are a bit like cats. By instinct they are curious and adventuresome. Even a pit toilet was interesting. As they grew up, the pit toilet lost its glitz. Today I am sure if the two-holers were in vogue, we would stop in town at the Texaco Service Station and be cautious about my grandchildren being curious. I think they would ask, "What is a pit toilet?" They might venture off to see for themselves. It is strange how exploring unique things can make children happy, even a two-holer pit toilet.

From their mother's point of view, sharing their visits to the pit toilet was another exhibit of bond and unity. Children don't really ask for much to make them happy. Sometimes just to allow them to satisfy their curiosity makes them happy.

Who Did It?

Most children are born programmed with four special words, "I didn't do it." Many times, I heard those same four words from all three of my children. In response I would say, "The dog must have done it." I would get a switch or belt and then look for the dog. One of them would rush to me sniffling and saying, "The dog didn't do it " and proceed to tell me the truth. They did not want the dog to get a whipping. I also hung a picture of Jesus Christ over the door seal in the living room. Occasionally I would say, "I was not here. Go tell Jesus Christ you didn't do it." It always worked; the guilty one would look at the picture and start crying while saying, "Momma, I didn't mean to do it." I taught them God and His son Jesus Christ could see all of our deeds, good and bad. Their respect for their Christian teaching made them unable to lie to the picture.

From their mother's point of view, children must be taught to revere and respect something of value. Jesus' picture kept them honest and reminded them that Jesus Christ wanted all children to be good and not lie. They could not lie to the picture of Jesus Christ. Thank you, God, for the revelation to use a picture to help instill honesty and truth. As adults they still won't lie; they are more willing to accept the consequences, good or bad, than to lie.

LaTrell Did It

When LaTrell was very small, she awakened and Ruby Dee did not hear her playing quietly. LaTrell took my pretty little pure linen molded straw hat and played cleaning the commode. Ruby Dee was hurt when she discovered LaTrell had sloshed it in and out of the commode's water. When I came home, Ruby Dee began to apologize. I knew that LaTrell was too young to have known better and Ruby Dee was not neglectful. Both were forgiven.

I knew it was easy for Ruby Dee not to have heard the quiet playing of a little girl less than five years old. I was disappointed about my hat because I had paid dearly for the hat to match a pure Irish linen suit that I copied and made from the elite Mr. Jack's showcase. The store did not have another hat like that special hat, but I lived without it and the incident became another funny memory.

From her mother's point of view, kids will be kids and

many children do unexplainable things out of innocence and curiosity.

Brian Did It

Once Brian shot a ballerina figurine off the wall with a slingshot. When I came home, I asked what happened to the ballerina. They giggled and told me that Brian had bet he was so good with a slingshot he could shoot between her legs and miss hitting her. He tried and missed. The figurine shattered off the wall. He was terrified for the rest of the day because he thought I would be very angry. When I arrived and saw the shattered figurine, I was upset. It was inexpensive, but it was the best we had for wall decorations, at the time. It was part of our pretty little stuff. They each took their turn making the story funny. Finally, they showed me how sharp Brian thought he was with a slingshot and how he looked when the ballerina shattered off the wall. It took plenty of time before I could laugh with them. When they finally made me laugh, it was funny.

From his mother's point of view, children are subject to try something they should not try. Brian thought he was good with the slingshot; obviously he wasn't. He had plenty of agony waiting for me to come home to discipline him about the figurine. The other two did not want to share his discipline. We kept the matching boy ballet figurine for a long time to remind Brian to not try his slingshot skills in the house. He did not get a spanking but he also never practiced target shooting in the house, again.

Garland Did It—Twice

One night, I hosted my Tomacdochi Club meeting and a member left her cigarette package under the sofa. Garland found the cigarettes the next day and decided to smoke. He lit a cigarette, laid it on a living room chair arm, and burned a hole in the chair's arm. He practiced an excuse on our neighbor Richard Soders. He told Richard that a rat had burned a hole in the chair's arm with a match. Richard told him, "Boy, if you have burned a hole in Myrt's chair, you are in trouble and she won't believe your rat lie." Garland went home dismayed and studied for another excuse. When I came home, I noticed a cover on the chair's arm. I pulled the cover back and asked who burned the chair. Brian and LaTrell knew nothing about the burn in the chair's arm. Garland said, "A black man in a brown car came looking for you and sat in the chair, went to sleep, and burned it. When he saw he had burned our chair, he got scared and left." Garland's story did not sound realistic, but he sounded truthful. I asked our neighbors about the black man and brown car. No one saw such. Richard Soders laughed and told me that Garland had tried one lie out on him and this was his new lie. We laughed and I went home. I made Garland smoke each of the remaining cigarettes and spanked him between each cigarette. I knew not to let him nor his sister and brother laugh about fire. Fire is too serious. After about six cigarettes, I asked if he had enough. He said, "I haven't finished them, yet." He finished smoking the cigarettes, as I became dizzy and watched. LaTrell and Brian did not tarry while he was getting his punishment. When he finished, Brian decided to tease him by saying, "Garland, do you still want to smoke?" Garland smiled and said, "No! I have kicked the habit." He jumped into the air and clicked his heels together, like they did on a television commercial for the Great American Smokeout.

From their mother's point of view, children will play or experiment with anything different. I never smoked and I guess the cigarettes piqued Garland's curiosity. In the midst of his punishment, he was still honest in that he kept smoking until he finished the pack. I had to give him a good spanking. He had to truly realize the danger of lighted cigarettes and fire. Neither Brian nor LaTrell tried to intervene. They knew that if Garland got a serious whipping, it had to be bad. It never happened again. Today, if anyone asks him if he smokes, he will happily say, "No! I kicked the habit when I was at the age of five." I think he may now be too heavy to jump and click his heels together, but he never desired smoking after that day. He really did kick the habit at the age of five.

From their mother's point of view, corporal punishment has its place when done in moderation. Garland got a clear message that fire is a real NO-NO!! Though Brian and Garland's bond was special, Brian knew that Garland needed discipline. He made no attempt to circumvent Garland's punishment.

Again, from their mother's point of view, I knew my teaching was working when I realized that both LaTrell and Brian could see that I was consistent and fair. They hated to see him being chastised, but neither disagreed with me over the issue of playing with fire.

Garland Is Drunk

Again, when Garland was about five years of age, he had a cold and decided to take some medicine. When LaTrell and Brian came from school, they noticed that Garland was exceptionally happy and playful. They also noticed he was hoarse, and he told them that he had taken some medicine. When I came home, Garland was extra happy to see me and was extremely playful with me, too. I thought his playfulness was excessive, but I did not think of his actions as being wrong. LaTrell and Brian were tickled at Garland and asked me what did I think was wrong with him. I laughed with them and wondered what was so funny. Brian showed me an empty Vick's 44 cough syrup bottle. They told me that Garland had decided to take the remainder of the cough syrup in order to get well quick. I asked Garland how he felt. He was full of play and laughter and cheerfully said, "Fine." Finally, it occurred to me that Garland was drunk on the alcohol in the cough syrup. I scolded him for taking an excessive amount of cough syrup. I explained the danger of his taking medicines without my permission. I made him drink a lot of water in an effort to dilute the syrup in his system. He was funny for several hours and finally went to sleep. He had a good night's sleep and no side effects from the Vick's 44.

From their mother's point of view, I never thought of keeping the Vick's out of reach because I always administered any and all medications. With that incident I learned that curious children will do what they see adults do, only without proper instructions. All children must be taught to not administer any kind of medicine.

Your Girlfriend Did It

Not too long after Garland's incident with the Vick's 44, my favorite girlfriend and I went to a nightclub. I never drank alcohol, but that night she insisted that I drink some beer. I did. Having drunk one can of beer, the world seemed to have completely changed and everything was funny. When she brought me home, I was still excessively happy and funny—better stated drunk, on less than two cans of beer. Brian smelled beer on my breath. He became so angry that he cried. He did not like the idea of my drinking beer at all. He wanted to know where and why did I drink some beer. I told him that she and I drank some beer at the nightclub. He was furious about my drinking beer. He called her and told her that I could not go out with her again if I had to drink beer. She was tickled because she could not believe that a child was so strong and verbal against his mother's drinking beer. I told her that they knew I hate drunkards, therefore they did not want me to drink even one beer. LaTrell and Garland did not like the idea either. However, they did not have to express their feelings because Brian was in total control.

From their mother's point of view, I was blessed to have a son who stood so firm on what he thought was best for me. He was totally right to have expressed his dismay, including the call to my friend. Though she and I thought it was funny for him to call her, it taught me that if children are taught good values, they have a right to expect their parents to adhere to the same rules that apply to the children. Thank you, Brian. I still do not drink alcohol of any kind.

Momma, We Did It

I never allowed my children to fight each other nor other children. However, boys will be boys. I once came home from work, and the boys met me at the car door.

They gleefully told me, "Momma, you won't like this, but we been fighting." They were full of smiles, laughter, and giggles. I asked, "Whom have you been fighting?" They happily said in unison, "Sonny." I was stunned because Sonny was one of their best little playmates. Brian explained that Sonny was unkind to Garland, and he could not let Sonny run over his little brother. I immediately began to think what did they do and how badly did they hurt Sonny. I asked them, "How is Sonny?" They laughed and said, "Oh, he is all right." They explained how Sonny had hollered to the other children, "Come get these Flakes brothers off me" and the fight was broken up without injury. Brian said, "Please take us to Uncle Boonie (my brother) so we can tell him we have been fighting."

I took them to my mother's house, and they were happy to tell my brother about the fight. My brother was proud of them for fighting. I watched the dynamics between all of them. Since Sonny was not hurt, I did not scold them. I could tell that it appeared natural for boys to want to fight. I insisted that fighting is not the best nor my method of problem solving. They knew my brother's and my ideas of right and wrong were very different. That is why they knew he would be impressed about them fighting. When the excitement and humor subsided, I talked with both of them about fighting. I explained that people can be hurt and loss of temper can cause death. They understood but remained proud that Brian had acted in defense of Garland and together they were the victors.

From their mother's point of view, there was a better way to solve their problem. Yet, a little person inside me felt good because my boys would not let others abuse either of them and surely not their sister.

Brian Did It—Hammerlock on Garland

Brian sometimes did big-brother teasing and gladly apologized to Garland for his mischievous deeds. Brian's sincere apologies were easy to accept, because he never wanted to hurt Garland's feelings. Garland always forgave anyone who hurt him, especially Brian. Garland was born humble and gentle, like his father. While wrestling, Brian once broke Garland's arm by putting a hammerlock on him as though they were professional wrestlers. LaTrell rushed to me in a loud, shrill cry, saying, "Momma, Brian has broken Garland's arm." I panicked and ran with her to check Garland's arm. She was right—the bone in his upper arm was actually broken through the whole bone. Garland was speechless and had a sad face. His arm was dangling in the middle of his upper arm. Immediately, I took him to Scott and White Memorial Hospital. The doctors took x-ray pictures and learned Garland had a bone cyst that needed corrective surgery. Brian was sad about hurting his little brother.

They had learned how to do the hammerlock from professional wrestlers. They loved wrestling and loved watching it on television with my mother. I took them to see many live wrestling matches of their favorite wrestlers. They wanted and I had bought us tickets in the first-class seats. One night, a wrestler slammed "The Brut's" head in the turnbuckle. A lot of snot, spit, blood, and sweat flew from "The Brut" and onto LaTrell. She frantically jumped up and shouted, "I don't ever want to sit this close again." Brian stood outside the arena by the door to see "The Brut" exiting. He screamed to me, "Momma, look, his boot is tall as me." I looked and he was right, "The Brut" was a huge man.

Back to Garland's broken arm, the doctors explained

that he needed to transplant bone from his pelvic area to his upper arm. The beauty in this awful experience is we could have not known about the cyst and later they might have had to amputate his arm. It would have been a tragedy for him to lose an arm simply out of not knowing it could have been corrected. All things work together for the good of those who love the Lord.

From their mother's point of view, all things thought to be bad may not be bad. They may be the beginning of something good. Thank God for Brian's hammerlock and "The Brut."

18

Becoming Teenagers

Babies do not come with an instruction guide, and no one has written a foolproof book on what to expect when rearing children. In their teenage years, rearing teenagers is a trial-and-error program for most parents. My being a single mother working more than thirty-two miles away from home made my challenge greater. The major lesson I demanded that they learn was being self-disciplined. I always taught them to discipline themselves because others could mistreat them before I could get home. I ***NEVER*** had to leave my job to discipline any of my children or at the school's request for my attention. The one thing for which I am most proud is their ability to be self-disciplined.

Their natural desires for nice things cost me more money than I can ever remember earning. I was forced to be frugal and thrifty in all our life needs. God blessed me with obedient children. God was not mad at me and He must have been in love with my children. For all the right reasons, He provided all of our needs.

Brian's Debut in Football

Brian and Garland liked and enjoyed watching and

playing sports. Brian was a young participant in sports. Every Saturday morning, LaTrell, Garland, and I went to see him play quarterback in the Little League games for the Boys' Club. I understood football, but I had forgotten the game plan is to kill the quarterback. When Brian called plays, the defensive linemen charged toward him. I panicked and loudly yelled, "Get off my boy." My children and other parents laughed at me for pacing along the sideline. We were very proud of their big brother playing quarterback. We had learned that being quarterback meant the coach thought that player was smart and could execute plays on the field and could think quickly when the game plan changed. Garland's pride in Brian made me extra proud, because I could see Brian's being smart enough to play quarterback made Garland happy, too.

I was a good Little League Mother. After their games I rushed around passing out packages of chocolate-filled cupcakes. The other parents noticed how happy it made the boys, and they began to alternate with bringing treats for the players.

From his mother's point of view, the cupcakes represented "reward" for playing a good game and being good little sportsmen. The cupcakes had nothing to do with winning or losing; they were incentive and encouragement for doing their best and demonstrating good character.

Garland's Debut in Basketball

Later, Garland wanted to play basketball for the Boys' Club. But, there was a serious shortage of men to coach the African-American boys' team. Bruce Etheridge, Garland's classmate, asked me to be their coach. I was very apprehensive about coaching boys at the Boys' Club; they (society) tended to reserve that role for men. I discussed my concerns about being a woman coaching boys. I feared the boys would be embarrassed by having a woman coach. Bruce said, "That's all right, Ms. Myrt. We will show them a woman can coach boys, too." That was such a profound statement from a serious little boy. I told them, "Let's go." Brian was my assistant coach and LaTrell served as our second driver. I had bought her a cute little white Ford Falcon station wagon. Our team was named Jack-in-the-Box, and it was a total family affair.

From their mother's point of view, I did whatever was necessary to be sure my children had a chance to do everything that they could to make them wholesome and become well-rounded adults. Brian and LaTrell's volunteering to help me meant their bond as siblings was important to each other. I knew that LaTrell and Brian's help meant they were anxious for "their baby—Garland" to have a chance to enjoy basketball at the Ralph Wilson's Boys' Club. I was happy to get off from work and go directly to the boys club to meet, practice, or play with my three children. It was late when we got home, but we were happy. They immediately began to do their homework while I prepared our meal. After late dinner, baths, and homework, we looked forward to the next day and a replay of our joy of another job well done.

Again, from their mother's point of view, being a woman coach for boys was a challenge and most rewarding. I rewarded and disciplined them by making them sit next to me when we rode home. Many members of our Jack-in-the-Box basketball team have achieved many meaningful successes in life. Bruce is head coach of Temple High School's varsity men basketball team. Thomas Taplin is a cross-country truck driver. Albert Reese was a

Super Bowl XXII (1987 season) championship Washington Redskins player and my son Garland is a senior warden. I am proud of all our team members, and I am most proud to have been a small part of their lives and maturation.

Once, Bruce was elbowed in the face during a game. My maternal instincts caused me to run, cuddle, and pet him on the floor. He was holding the ball and his nose was bleeding. I cradled his head in my arm and cleaned his sweaty little face that was smeared with blood. Bruce looked at me and begged, "Ms. Myrt, may I take my free throw?" My motherly instinct was tempted to say, "No." My better judgment and competitive spirit spoke out, "Yes, baby, go take your free throws and make them good." I gave him a serious smack of encouragement on his rear end, and he made his two free throws. For many years and many times, I have recalled that incident with Bruce. One day he said, "Ms. Myrt, won't you please forget that?" My answer was, "No, life is going to bloody your nose again and again, and you are going to have to get back in the game to take and make your free throws." Bruce thought about the lesson in that scenario and what I meant. He replied, "Ms. Myrt, you are right. Life has already bloodied my nose and I did take my free throws. You are right, Ms. Myrt, now I see what you mean. I am sure my nose will bleed again and I will make my free throws." We both laughed because we had adopted another winner's concept and attitude.

From the team's coach/mother point of view, I taught the team that each time life made their nose bleed, wipe it off, regain their composure, and make their free throws. Secondly, for my own sons and as coach of the Jack-in-the-Box's point of view, I taught them to never let anything deter you, be resilient. Place your feet on the free throw line, focus your mind and eyes on the net, put your hands in good position, and make all your free throws.

Brian Sings and LaTrell Dances

Brian wanted to sing with the elite and costly Temple Boy's Choir and LaTrell wanted to dance with the Margaret Newcombe's School of Ballet. I don't remember how I afforded meeting their desires, but I did and was happy to do so. We all dressed appropriately and went to of each of their performances, to include going out of town. Brian wore a pretty little red wool blazer with an Ivy League emblem on the pocket with white shirt and black bow tie. He wore black pants, shoes and socks. They sang to open a concert for the Vienna Boys Choir and entertained the Governor of Texas. Brian was happy to get a Certificate of Appreciation from the Governor of Texas. One of the chaperons enjoyed telling me about the security around the boys in the choir. I had little respect for her conversation because I could pick up Brian and take him home while neither the director nor the chaperon realized we had left.

LaTrell was the only African-American girl in her school of ballet. She wore her hair pulled back in to a bow, a pretty little pink tutu, and hard-toed ballet slippers. She had the grace and flow of the wind. Her brothers and I kept smiles on our faces as she whirled on her toes, leaped across the stage, and landed on the opposite side of the stage with the grace of a swan. When the audience smiled and looked at us, we knew she had done well and we were proud to be her support team.

We Followed the Wildcats

We followed David President, Mae Mae's youngest son, to all of his football games, no matter the weather or distance. One night we went to Corsicana to see the Temple High School Wildcats and David play football. David was a great player and wore the family's traditional number 88. At a football game in Corsicana, Texas, it rained so hard and long that when I raised my arm to cheer, the rain ran down my sleeve into my armpits. One of my children said they wanted to use the toilet. I told them, "No one will know the difference; let it go." When the game was over, we ran to the car. I turned on the heater and told my children to undress to their underwear and so did I. The car heater kept us warm. We prayed that no policeman would stop me for any reason. We made it home without incident, thanks to God. God probably laughed at us.

We were equally as devoted to David's basketball games. David was an all-around athlete and watching him play was a pleasure. I bought LaTrell a huge mum corsage with #88 for the homecoming game. David was happy because he liked her as he would have loved a little sister.

From their mother's point of view, following David was a major part of their bonding process. David's being their godmother's son made him very important to all of us. Their cheering for David enhanced LaTrell, Brian, and Garland's bonding with each other while also feeling that David represented a bigger brother. They knew I was teaching them to love and support those who loved and supported them. Bonding and loving does not happen by osmosis; it has to be taught. Love and bonding outside the family helped my children to grow up and genuinely care for people regardless of what others have to offer. Following the Temple Wildcats events taught them the spirit of loyalty. I loved my segregated education of Dunbar, and they loved Temple High. Character comes from belonging to something special and that something special caring about you, in return.

Brian and Garland's Basketball Games

Brian played sports in Lamar Junior High School and a little in high school. Brian was exciting to watch as he played basketball. He moved swiftly and had a lot of natural body movements to be envied. He could dribble with both hands and shift the ball from left to right before the opponent could realize he had changed hands. Garland watched Brian with amazement, admiration and adoration. Garland played basketball in Lamar Junior and Temple High Schools. Brian helped Garland at the Boys' Club, to improve his game and techniques in handling the ball. Brian attended Garland's games and cheered him to victory. Garland enjoyed making Brian happy at everything they shared. Brian would scream, "That's my boy, go, baby," as if Garland was his son. Some people knew Garland was Brian's brother and loved to hear Brian cheer for Garland. At everything they enjoyed, they were each other's best fans. I cheered for both of them, no matter when and how well they performed.

From their mother's point of view, healthy competitive sports are good for children to learn, play, and watch. Learning how to win and lose generally helps adults accept defeat and be a jubilant winner. As a child, I participated in many competitive activities. Sports enhanced the principles of healthy competition, which helped when

I was forced to face prejudice and discrimination. I always knew I had a chance to win the next game or in the next season. I knew how to practice and prepare for the next meet, and very few could beat me in the next game. Children need to be taught the value of good and healthy competition, which also builds character. It helps them work through the mazes of life.

From their mother's point of view, the rewards of my competitive spirit taught me to encourage them to be tough and fearless competitors and how to deal with defeat. My children's bond became more profound as they savored victory together.

Civic Involvement

Garland And Momma Are N.A.A.C.P. Presidents

During the time I was president of the Temple branch of the National Association for the Advancement of Colored People (N.A.A.C.P.), my children were active in the youth council. We enjoyed being on programs and going to the various N.A.A.C.P. conventions. Garland was elected President of the N.A.A.C.P. Youth Council. He demonstrated leadership and organizational skills, which made Brian proud to say, "When I grow up, I want to be just like my little brother." Brian's accolades made Garland happy and proud to do his work as a leader. Garland liked his big brother's pride in his ability to conduct meetings. He learned *Robert's Rules of Order* by visiting International Training in Communication with me and watching me conduct meetings of the Adult Branch of N.A.A.C.P. and other social and civic organizations.

Brian marveled over Garland's ability to accomplish important things through others and making good decisions. He bragged about Garland's leadership ability. He knew Garland was a future leader and always encouraged him to do his best and more. Their bonding was at its best.

From their mother's point of view, I was happy to see my sons' concern for the well-being of people who were treated unfairly and to have compassion for people who are less fortunate. Simply stated, I was proud of "the Flakes boys." Garland loved the N.A.A.C.P. programs. He went to the national convention in St. Louis in 1976 and Miami Beach in 1980. He won Mr. Freedom for Temple and State of Texas N.A.A.C.P. in 1980, and second place in the National Mr. Freedom contest in Miami Beach in 1980, and won a college scholarship from the N.A.A.C.P. in 1981.

Garland competed and won awards in the Optimist Oratorical Contest. Again, Brian bragged about Garland's many accomplishments and encouraged him to keep doing well. Each time Garland did something great, Brian found a way to give him special congratulations, which encouraged Garland to undertake additional challenges. Brian once gave me a pretty trophy, which states "Most Important Woman In My Life—My Mother." In retrospect, Brian has always been a special guy to all of us, in his own special way. Brian's pleasant personality makes him easy to love.

From their mother's point of view, when one child does well and the others applaud or support their efforts, both children grow as a unit and share the victory. Such growth and support is special bonding between siblings. Such bonding nullifies sibling rivalry.

Buy a Chevrolet and See California

In 1971 my mother promised my children that she would buy another car for me to drive us to California. As time drew closer for the trip, my mother began to vacillate regarding buying a car and taking the trip. I asked her to be certain about her promise or I would buy a car and take my children to Los Angeles. My mother smirked and told me, ". . . You ain't got no money to buy a car," and she added her smug laughter. I told her, "I don't lie to my children, and I will buy a car and take them to California." My mother reneged and I made plans to buy us a car for the trip. In spring of 1972, I visited the used car dealership of Mr. T. I. Whiteley and Sons. I liked a light gold 1970 Impala Chevrolet, four door hardtop, air-conditioned car with leather seats. It was beautiful to me. I told Mr. Whiteley that I needed to get my children's approval or disapproval. Mr. Whiteley was amazed and said he never had a customer who cared if their children liked or disliked a car before they made their final decision. He said, "Drive the car home and take your children for a ride." I did and they loved it too. They were happy. I always valued their opinions in any major decisions. I made arrangements to buy the car for our trip to California. Immediately, I had an eight-track tape player installed under the driver's seat.

Rosa Fulcher went with us to Los Angeles. En route we slept in a motel in Carlsbad, New Mexico, and visited the Carlsbad Caverns. We listened to Bill Withers's Smiling Faces and lots of Barry White on the eight-track tape under the front seat. In Los Angeles, we visited family members, friends, and spent time sight-seeing. We went to the grand opening of the Magic Mountain amusement park and saw Pat Boone and his famous white shoes. We took a friend to Disneyland. We nicknamed the friend "the little ol'lady from Pasadena." Our cousin Opal Buckner, Unk's youngest daughter, also went with us to Disneyland in Anaheim, California.

At Disneyland, we saw Diana Ross and the Supremes. The crowd for the Supremes was huge. I told my children that people will be kind and nice to smart and polite children. I told them to hold hands, LaTrell in front, then Brian, and last Garland. I coached LaTrell to touch the person in front of her and say, "Excuse me, please." I coached Garland to say, "Thank you." I coached them to smile nicely and keep moving until they moved to the front. I coached Brian to stay in the middle and hold their hands. I told them when the show was over not to try to come back to me but to stay at the front of the huge crowd. When the show was over, I went down front to find them. They had held hands, smiled, and worked the crowd. They worked our plan all the way to the very first row. When I was able to reach them, they had three front-row seats. I was very proud of them because they had followed my instructions and proved that some strangers will be kind to nice children.

From their mother's point of view, when children follow wise instructions and stay focused, they can accomplish any of their heart's desires. Getting so close to Diana Ross and the Supremes is still the dream of millions. As they grew I loved watching them talking, walking, skipping, and playing together. Often, they held hands to ensure all were safe; that made my heart smile. I made them lots of look-alike play clothes. LaTrell tended to stay close to me; she was my best little friend. She and her brothers cherished each other. She and Brian share a unique and strong bond, not to be taken lightly. They were the big children, and both were born under the sign of Taurus, whatever that may mean. Garland was all of our baby; he is five years younger than LaTrell. Brian is actually the hub of our wheel and keeps all of us rolling together. We respected his being the man of the house.

From their mother's point of view, there is nothing more comforting than knowing my children love and care for each other. Sibling rivalry is a pain I have lived with daily and I refuse to allow my children to experience it.

In Our Chevrolet We Saw the U.S.A.

After our trip to Los Angeles, annually, we took vacations and enjoyed seeing America. I allowed the boys to pay our hotel/motel bills; this task gave them a sense of manhood. All of them ordered room service. They swam in beautiful hotel and motel swimming pools. They read highway maps and actually helped to decide the route we would travel. They helped to decide what side attractions we would visit while traveling. They enjoyed making adult decisions and consequently broadened their perspectives and outlook about life. They liked sharing the opportunity to see America and sharing conversations that I did not hear. They were bonding in ways that I did not know.

During our many trips, we saw James Brown and Chaka Khan. The Hemisphere, Six Flags of Texas and Over Mid-America, Carlsbad Caravans, Petrified Forest, Indianapolis 500 Race Track, and a United States Mint in Denver. Circus Circus Casino in Las Vegas, Hoover Dam, San Francisco sights, San Diego Zoo, visited skiing resorts in Vale Colorado, Pike's Peak, Gardens of the Gods, and other mountains in Colorado. We visited the Royal Gorge near Colorado Springs, museums and Olde Town in Chicago. Detroit sights and a trip to Canada to see Uncle Tom's Cabin. We visited the historical home of Booker T. Washington in Diamond, Missouri. We visited and saw the docked luxury ocean liner *Queen Mary* in California. One summer we visited Texas only and saw many historical markers in Texas history. We toured battle ship *Texas* and rode a ferry boat from Louisiana to Texas. We went to Breckenridge Zoo in San Antonio, and Busch Gardens in Houston. We visited an Indian reservation in Livingston, Texas. We shared the first year's opening of Astro World with my high school classmate Rozena Pride Jordan and her children. We enjoyed many other exciting and educational places and experiences. People at Fort Hood often said military children were smarter than others because of their exposure to different cultures and travels. I felt compelled to expose my children and let them travel so they would be smarter, too. It worked.

Each of our trips gave us a chance to learn, to laugh, to run, and to play, and to grow intellectually together. We took pictures and ate in fancy restaurants together. They ordered from menus just like adults. I allowed them to buy their back-to-school clothes while we traveled throughout the United States. Their back-to-school clothes were part of their souvenirs from the respective cities and were memoirs of our trips. In California, Brian picked two shirts for himself and Garland. The shirts had ruffles down the front. They literally wore those shirts to shreds. Brian loved to say, "I bought this shirt in California."

From their mother's point of view, God was always near and taking care of us as we traveled. When Garland was eleven, he loved to tell people, "I have been in more states than I am old." When he first said that, I thought it was just cute. Afterwards I thought that was something very special and something many people could not truthfully say. God taught me how to manage my meager earnings in order to provide the best for my children, and He kept us safe over thousands of miles of travel. We had a minor wreck in Indiana, a large truck backed over the trunk of our car. We faced a mighty lightning storm in the deserts of New Mexico; there was no place to hide. He kept us safe in a rain storm and flood in Alabama; we found shelter in a hospital lobby. I almost got a traffic ticket and sent to jail in Chicago. We experienced blatant racism and rejection for lodging in Pocahontas, Illinois. God could not have been mad at me; he actually traveled with us. Thank you, GOD, for being our ever present and unseen pilot. Always in the midst of danger, I think he was saying, "Peace, be still."

In Chicago's Old Towne, Brian quickly noticed the poverty-stricken black community was directly behind the sights of the renovated Olde Town. He said to me, "Momma, I see what you want us to learn. Now let's get out of here." For the first time in his life, he saw hungry children eating from trash dumpsters. My children became more appreciative of their lives and of what I provided. They were saddened when we visited Southside Chicago and saw very old people sitting outside with keys around their necks to the front door of their high-rise apartments, another key to the elevator, and two more keys to their individual apartments. At that time crime had not crippled nor home-bounded the senior citizens in Temple, Texas. We had never seen senior citizens at risk and ill-respected. We were saddened for the aged citizens.

He Looked Cute

Once in the car, Garland took a flash photo of Brian while we were riding. We were surprised and asked him, "Why did you waste the film?" He looked sad and said, "Brian looked so cute sitting in the corner of the seat I just wanted a picture of him." We laughed. When the pictures were developed, he was right. Brian was sitting on his knees with his arms wide spread and wearing a big smile. His face looked so healthy and happy, he was cute. How lovely. Garland just wanted to capture that appearance of his brother. That was another act that proved they were soulfully bonded. It also showed how deeply he loved Brian. That picture is very special to all of us because of the story that surrounds it and Brian's big smile.

All three children spent many hours and days talking about and looking at their vacation pictures. They love recalling the things that they enjoyed and learned while travelling. They grew together and enjoyed sharing and showing their photo albums with friends and telling the joys of their experiences.

From their mother's point of view, these three children had personal experiences together that can never be duplicated. There was nothing more exciting and rewarding than to see them growing, learning, and traveling together. There was no better way to spend money than to enrich their lives and broaden their sphere of reference. Our travels made them more learned than children whose experiences were limited to our humble neighborhoods in the city of Temple, Texas.

Their Education Becomes More Serious

Brian's eleventh-grade school year was filled with negative peer pressures. I learned that Brian was skipping school. Garland was very unhappy because he wanted Brian to finish high school and college. When Garland learned something was distracting Brian's attention from school and their home training, he began to worry. I discussed with Brian the issue of his skipping school. I spent serious time and energy convincing Brian that I would not tolerate his lost of interest in his public school education.

At the end of the 1976 school year, Brian asked for a job. I told him, "I have made arrangements for your summer job." He was happy but was disappointed when he learned that I meant he was going to summer school. In the summer of 1976, I insisted and he went to summer school. Garland and I went to a National N.A.A.C.P. convention in St. Louis, and Brian overslept on the day of final examination, shucks! He did not get credit for the class and there was no financial refund. Garland and I were hurt. Garland was hurt because he was looking forward to Brian's catching up with his schoolwork.

The following September, I visited Mrs. Molly Smith, senior counselor, on the first day of school. She reviewed his transcript and said, "If he passes a full load of subjects, he will still need four additional subjects, shucks!" I asked her to enroll Brian in four correspondence courses in order for him to graduate in 1978. She did and I monitored his completion of the four courses while he carried a full load of classroom studies. I awakened him at 5:30 A.M., when I was preparing for work. I brought him home from the basketball court at 6:00 P.M. to study each evening. He was not always happy when I made him study instead of allowing him to play basketball. His education was my number-one priority, and it became his number one. Garland watched my unyielding determination for Brian's studies to be successful. I placed suspense dates on his correspondence courses and reviewed his tests before mailing them to the school. We were happy when he told us the school had certified his completing the four correspondence courses and he had enough credits for graduation.

Mrs. Smith was elated because she had told me the average child could only complete two correspondence courses in one year, never four. We recalled that I told her, "You said, the average child and I said my child." I did not know that Mrs. Smith had told Superintendent William Valigura about Brian and my efforts to ensure his graduation. She told Mr. Valigura of our success, and he applauded Brian and me, because we had proved, when a parent, child, and counselor work together, children can be successful at any undertaking. As graduation drew nearer, Brian became happier about his accomplishments. I bought him some last-minute graduation invitations; he was excited. Many people gave him lovely graduations gifts; he told me, "Momma, I didn't know graduation is like Christmas." He calls his diploma "our high school diploma." Garland was excited and happy about his brother's high school graduation.

Brian Goes to College

During the summer after Brian's graduation, Garland went to Temple Junior College and enrolled in night school classes in Brian's name. Garland wanted desperately for Brian to go to college. Garland knew Brian was naturally smart and has a tremendous natural ability to learn. The bond that existed between them would not let Garland accept Brian's not furthering his education. Garland asked Brian to go with him to the Public Health Clinic to get a health card for serving food at the Temple City Parks and Recreation. As they waited, the nurse called for Brian to come in and get a shot. Brian was surprised, but with Garland's encouragement, he took the shot. Brian questioned Garland's enrolling him in college. Garland explained to Brian that he wanted him to become a successful and learned man. Brian could hardly wait for me to come home from work to tell me what Garland had done.

Upon my arrival, Brian looked at me, thought, and said, "You already know, you gave Garland the money to enroll me in Temple Junior College." I smiled and then he knew. Garland and I had joined together to send him to college. Garland was happy and Brian understood that it was out of love for him that we had conspired against him.

Brian made excellent grades, but at the end of that semester, he told both of us, "Don't try this again, because I am not going back." I told him, "I have destroyed another myth, 'you can take a horse to water, you can make him drink, stick his nose under the water, but you cannot control how much he will swallow.'" Garland and I agreed to not push him into college the next semester. Garland knew that he had made a significant contribution toward helping his brother do what we thought was best for his future.

From their mother's point of view, when a younger brother goes that far for his older brother, it was worth the money for the possibility that Brian could have continued a quest for higher education. I told Brian in his next effort for advance education, he would have to pay for it himself. I have kept that promise. However, I did help him to get a grant to a business school in Dallas. He did very well academically, but a misfortune interrupted the completion of his studies.

Garland Focuses on His Educational Interests

Garland was in the tenth grade and focusing on his educational future and being president of the N.A.A.C.P. Youth Council. He played varsity basketball very well and became one of its captains and strongest players. Coach Don Brownlee told Garland that he wanted him to become an intimidator. Garland asked me what that meant. I had not allowed them to fight. Therefore he did not have a relationship that involved intimidation. Quickly, with my fist, I hit him in his chest, hard. It really hurt him, both physically and emotionally.

Painfully, he asked, "Momma, why did you do that to me?" I told him to never let anyone else do that to him again. I related it to what Coach Brownlee meant. He quickly understood that being a center post man meant taking and staying in control of his area. He returned to the game and became a tough competitor and a real fierce intimidator. Though my hitting him served its purpose, it hurt me too. I never wanted to inflict pain on my children because I had too much experience with pain from both my mother and brother. Garland's rapid growth made him a strong 6'3" healthy center post with an enormous arm spread and an intimidator to be feared. Brian was working and watching Garland play high school basketball as often as he could. Brian's face beamed with love when he cheered and said, "That's my baby." They were still growing and bonding. They always hugged and shared a holy kiss when they saw each other. To date that has not changed. After Garland's high school graduation, their mutual personal interests began to wane.

From their mother's point of view, when parents teach and plant seeds of bonding, siblings grow stronger and closer as they age and that builds unparalleled character. However, we must continually nurture their bond.

19

Adulthood

Brian Has a Son

On December 1, 1979, Brian's girlfriend delivered a son, Keith KaZell. His middle name, KaZell, is for Garland KaZell and my father's brother. Though Brian asked her to marry him, she opted to not marry. I diligently bought nice things for the baby. His mother told me that her boyfriend did not want me coming to her mother's house to leave bags for the baby without calling first. I assured her the next time I would call before I would come. Shortly after Keith's birth, she married another young man. That fall, Brian's father, Mr. Right Soldier Retired, drove from Tampa, Florida to see his grandson. The woman's husband would not let Mr. Right Soldier Retired see the baby. Her husband came to my home while we were having dinner to tell me that Mr. Right Soldier Retired could not see his grandson. I was angered and tried to physically attack the young man in my front yard. Brian heard my anger toward the young man and came outside. Brian squelched what was becoming a nasty scene between the young man and me. Brian was angered by the young man's disrespect for me at my home. Brian ordered the young man away from our home and told him to never return.

From a grandmother's point of view, it was hard to cope with being told to call before I came. My feelings were hurt. I was hurt because I knew how often before conception she called my home late at night to talk to Brian. I knew I had taken her to get a lemon pie from Jack-in-the-Box after 2:00 A.M. to satisfy her cravings. I knew Brian worked very hard and prepaid all of Keith's and his mother's hospital bills. It was hard to accept her little insolent husband's boldness when he came to my home and confronted me while denying us the right to see the baby. I was not a very good example for my family when I was raging at the young man in my front yard. My family knew her husband was being a jerk and was being unfair and disrespectful to me at my home. Again, I wanted to rumble.

From their mother's point of view, it was clear she wanted to have a baby by Brian. Yet it was selfish to not share the baby with our family. From their mother's point of view, there are some things that we cannot control, but we can control our response. Self-control also helps to build strong character.

Brian Goes to Houston

Brian got a job with Dane's Wholesale Distributor, in Temple, Texas, and was promoted to a better job in Houston. He made pretty good money and lived in his own apartment. Garland was happy because his brother was doing quite well. Brian's intelligence was quickly recognized and rewarded by Dane's supervision, and he was promoted to a Retail Merchandise Specialist. This position had a high degree of trust and responsibility. He had a company van, a company credit card, and a route to serve that was not in the core of Houston's toughest community. Unfortunately, he had not matured enough for the degree of trust, independence, and responsibility the position required.

While he was in Houston, my cousin, Cleo Thornton, was proud to have him to visit her home. She and her children had enjoyed taking care of him when I commuted to keypunch school, in Houston, therefore he was special to her family. While in this position, he had serious surgeries on his feet. His absence of work, while his feet were healing, gave him time to see things that his work kept him too busy to see. Those things were not good for him and were detrimental to his future. In fact they were his first major negative distractions. He did so well that he invited Garland to visit him in Houston. Garland was sixteen and drove our green van to visit Brian for a week. Brian was ecstatic to have his "my baby" visit him. He took Garland to a live musical concert, and they had a lot of fun. They did several nice educational and entertaining things together.

I had second thoughts. My maternal instincts were concerned about sixteen-year-old Garland's driving to Houston alone and finding his way to Brian's apartment. Garland had no problem and enjoyed being trusted to make the trip to see his brother. Brian took good care of his little brother, though Garland had grown a lot taller than Brian. Garland had a marvelous time with Brian. Their bond inspired Brian to host his brother in the big city of Houston. Garland says, "Brian did not allow me to spend any money. He took total care of me during my visit." Their bonding was at its best.

Later, after a series of bad decisions, Brian lost his

job with Dane's. He lost sight of his goals and began to drift. Garland painfully worried about Brian. Brian moved and began to do battle with Dallas. Both Dallas and Brian won a round each. Eventually, Dallas began winning many rounds in a row. Garland's worry about Brian's safety in Dallas became more intense and hurt me to see his pain for his brother. Garland knew Dallas was a big vicious city, full of crime and danger. Brian began shuffling from job to job and from one bad decision to another bad decision. He was moving from one bad place of dwelling to another. He began to lose jobs, and the temptation of drugs and vice of drug addiction began to overrule his better judgment. Garland and I prayed.

Garland Goes to College

Despite their difference in decisions, they kept close contact with each other even though Brian had moved back to Houston and later again to Dallas. Garland graduated from Temple High School and was attending Texas Lutheran College (TLC) in Seguin, Texas, studying and playing ball. Some friends, Brian, LaTrell, and I loaded into my green van and went to Austin to see Garland and TLC play against Huston-Tillotson College. We shopped and ate in the mall and agreed to meet at the van at 6:30 P.M. for us to go to the basketball gym. Brian was shopping in the mall and was late to meet us at the van. I left him and he caught a ride to Huston-Tillotson.

LaTrell was furious with me for leaving Brian. I knew Brian would finish his shopping and join us at the ball game. I also, understood LaTrell's unrest because her bonding with her brothers was strong and precious, too. The party of us cheered for TLC. Garland's college life was going great, and he began to establish goals, priorities, and dreams for his professional future. He aspired to become a statewide elected official. During one visitation home, Brian sarcastically said to Garland, "What you got to say, college boy?"

Garland was hurt and painfully told me, "It seems my college education is going to cost me my brother's love." I told Garland to not pay any attention to such statements because his light was green and all of his arrows were pointing upward. I told him, "Brian's red light is self-imposed and the result of his poor decisions." I remind him that a red light is only on for a short time and it turns to green again. Garland seemed to accept my analogy, but he remained sad. I continued to help Garland cope with the pains of his brother's mistakes. I stood in the gap between them.

Their bond is very important to Garland and no less to Brian. In Garland's senior year of college, he transferred to Huston-Tillotson College in Austin, Texas. TLC wanted to redshirt him, but he refused to stay in TLC for five years just to play basketball longer. He said "I did not come to college to become a Kareem Abdul-Jabbar. I want my degree and an opportunity to get a good job."

From their mother's point of view, all children are not the same and they think differently. When they become adults, they make choices, some according to their parental teaching and their life experiences. A painful reality is that when they have made their choices, they have to live with the results of their choices, regardless of whether they are good or bad. It was tough but I learned that I don't have to take guilt trips for their shortcomings.

Garland Gets Married

On December 22, 1984, Garland married Delena Kay Johnson of Killeen, Texas. Garland's bond with his brother meant his brother must be the best man, and Brian's son, Keith KaZell, the ring bearer. Garland knew Brian was making some bad decisions and not taking the best of care of himself. That did not matter as much as Garland's desire for his brother to be the best man in his formal wedding. The sight of those brothers and Keith KaZell in white tuxedo suits, could not have been better. My greatest joy was Garland's wanting his brother to be his best man and Brian's being proud to do so. My mother and brother attended, as did my life mentor, Mrs. B. Kay Hornsby. Rev. A. C. Sutton and James Smith of San Antonio attended and videotaped the wedding. Many of our precious friends of Temple also came to Fort Hood, Texas, to share that blessed occasion. Joy was in the air.

From their mother's point of view, I had done what was right and it had worked. My heart fluttered as LaTrell and I were being escorted to our seats. We wore gorgeous lookalike lavender dresses. My heart thanked God, because there before me stood the three most important men in my life. My first son, my baby son, and my first grandson; they looked good to me. I looked at my beautiful daughter in a dress that I had made by her choice. I thanked God for never being mad at me. I thanked Him for being extra good to me and my family and for His continual blessings being with and upon us. Love filed the air.

From their mother's point of view, their bond was clearly locked in cement and little Keith KaZell was learning what his uncle and dad meant to each other.

Keith KaZell was also learning how much his Uncle Garland loved him and how his dad's family loved each other.

Garland Graduates from College

In May 1985, Garland graduated from Huston-Tillotson college in Austin, Texas, with his bachelor's degree. His major was Political Science and his minor was Government, the bases for an aspiring politician. Brian was living in Dallas, came to Temple, and joined us in going to Garland's college graduation. Brian's comment was, "I had to come see my little brother graduate from college." Brian was as happy and proud of Garland as if he had graduated from college himself. Again, another demonstration of love and the strong bond between two loving brothers. My mother did not want to attend. Mrs. B. Kay Hornsby went and shared this blessed occasion, too. Rev. A. C. Sutton and James Smith of San Antonio also shared this blessed event. It was a day of jubilance and excitement for Garland's having reached another major plateau.

From their mother's point of view, these brothers loved each other and their sister no matter what choices the other one made. I thanked God for showing me how to teach siblings to love each other.

Garland Has a Daughter

On May 26, 1985, Garland's wife presented us with a darling little girl, Brittany. To Brian, Brittany was the most precious and prettiest baby girl whom he had ever seen and held. He loved being her uncle and her being his niece. Brian called Garland often to ask how his little niece was doing. Regardless of what Brian was doing, he came home to see his brother's baby. When Brittany began to talk, Brian was ecstatic when she would say, "Uncle Byyynn." To Brian, Brittany was the most darling gift that an uncle could ever hope to have and hold.

From their mother's point of view, the bond was being past onto the next generation and it could not get any better than that, I thought. Life had shown me that real love gets better day by day.

During one of their visitations, we went to Long John Silver's fish house. Brian rushed to get one of the sea captain's hats for Brittany. He thought she was the prettiest little sea sailor that he had ever seen. I relished in his joy and excitement over his brother's baby. I watched Garland. His face was filled with happiness as he watched his brother enjoy his baby girl. I watched Brian's face filled with smiles as his hands were holding and bouncing his little niece. I watched Kay as she watched my sons. What could I say? Nothing. It kept getting better. I felt a special sense of love for them because they were demonstrating the results of what I tried to do the most, teach my children how to love each other. Children don't come with written instructions, and rearing them is not an exact science. Rearing them is a trial-and-error process. I thank God for marching me through the lonely and challenging journey of single parenting.

Garland Goes to Work

After Garland's graduation, he told me that he needed a job. I told him that I was not like some white man who makes his son a vice-president of the bank and lives happily ever after. We laughed. I told him that I did have some influence and maybe I could help. He smiled. I asked if he would work for the Texas Department of Corrections (TDC). He said, "Yes, I want to work and take care of my family." I contacted a personnel employee and asked about the process of gaining employment in TDC. I asked for help to get my son a job. I was told, "If your son needs a job, send him to me." I did and Garland proved mature, educationally prepared, and physically worthy of being hired and went through the academy. His first job with TDC was "rolling bars." I asked many questions in order to understand that "rolling bars" meant the duties of a Correctional Officer. He was willing to do anything and everything to do a good job. He began to study the system's promotion program. His first goal was to make Warden in ten years. Brian thought Garland's going to work at TDC was good, but he said, "I could not like that kind of work." Garland said, "Someone has to do it, and I see the potential of a career within the TDC system." I admired his being goal oriented and willing to pursue a career rather than just settling for a job.

From their mother's point of view, it is okay for siblings to think differently. It's okay for them to like and want different things out of life. Everything that is different is not bad. I knew their different choices for work would not infringe on their bond.

Different Lives and Close Bonds

Life and the many responsibilities that came with beginning a family caused Garland to spend every waking hour adjusting to his new job, life as a provider for his family, and settling into living in a new city. Brian and

Garland were not able to see each other as often as they wanted. They were committed to tell each other hello and show expressions of love for each other. They used the telephone to nurture their bond.

In 1986 the Temple Branch of N.A.A.C.P. gave me an appreciation program, at Mount Zion Missionary Baptist Church. Each of my children was present. The Superintendent of the Temple School District, Marilyn Hoster, stole the heart of our little Brittany, and they spent the evening playing together. Brian and Garland sat next to each other to share this blessed event. LaTrell gave the words of appreciation for my children. As I sat in the reception room, I saw a lady staring, with a grimace. I asked what she saw. She looked smug and simply shrugged her shoulders to say "I don't know." I looked and saw two men hugging. I told her, "Those are my sons, they hug and kiss each other whenever they greet and leave each other's presence." She was astonished and said, "I have five brothers and I have never seen any of them hug." I gave that some serious thought. Sweetly it brought to my remembrance that they had been taught to love each other, even in public. Their bond is so real and deep they don't mind showing love for each other, even in public. Thanks to God, that has not changed.

From their mother's point of view, it is great and beautiful when brothers love each other and have learned to love each other so strongly that they don't mind public demonstration of their love. Their love for each other is beautiful enough to climax all my motherly dreams.

They Begin to Shape Their Lives

Garland's life began taking shape as a father, husband, correctional officer, and spiritual leader at Greater Zion Missionary Baptist Church in Huntsville, Texas, and as a good and active citizen, in the City of Huntsville. Brian was living in Dallas and searching for the pieces to make his life whole. Garland could foresee a career with TDC and began to mentally map his way from Correctional Officer to Warden. Brian's life was in turmoil with temporary employment, a temporary relationship with a nice woman, and a sick serious hunger for drugs, which haunted his body and mind. Garland and I prayed for Brian.

One Christmas they met at home, 411 South 32nd Street, the home where love was taught, nurtured, and maintained. They met and greeted each other with a hug and a holy kiss. Brian was happy and showed how much he loved being an uncle to Garland's two daughters, Brittany and Chaundra. Garland equally enjoyed being uncle to Brian's son, Keith KaZell. Keith's middle name, KaZell, is for Garland's middle name from my father's brother. KaZell is a third-generation name in my father's family. Their conversations were providing positive reinforcement to each other's lives. Later, they spoke with each other, in privacy. That was a conversation to which I was rightfully not privy. During dinner, Brittany told her daddy, "When I grow up, I want to live next door to Uncle Brian." Both of them relished the innocence of that small child. I smiled deep down inside; she was expressing love for her daddy's brother. Brian told me, "What a challenge and precious desire for a little girl to want to live next door to me, her father's brother."

From their mother's point of view, what greater compliment could the whole family have than for a tiny little girl to love her uncle so much. Clearly, she had learned her daddy and his brother love each other. That began character building in Brittany.

We Need to Paint Mom's House

My sons' lives began to drift further apart. They were living apart and focusing on whatever was important to their separate agendas. More time slipped between their shared visits. When my home needed painting, they made plans to come home on a certain day and do the painting. On a bright Friday evening, they met and planned the painting for the weekend. Brian painted the lower part, and Garland stood on the ladder and painted the higher part. While they were painting the same area, they talked brother bonding talk. These were conversations for which I was not privy. When they reached trimming paint, they shared it and kept moving. My neighbors and passersby slowed down to see the brothers painting their mother's home. Some called me to say, "It is beautiful to see your sons painting your home." I felt good with each call; some said that they could not get their son(s) to do such a favor. I could only tell the callers that God had blessed me so much that my sons enjoyed painting my home.

From a mother's point of view, their painting my home symbolized success in my trying to nurture mutual love and respect among my children. I thanked God for my sons being willing to make time to help me. Upon completion of their work and when it was time for them to return to their destinations, little Brittany put the icing on the cake, again. She said to Brian, "Uncle Brian, thanks for coming and helping my dad paint Num Num's house." Again, we were extremely shocked and happy about the words that came from the lips of such a precious little girl.

From their mother's point of view, Brittany showed that she saw and understood the love and bond that existed between her dad and his brother and their love for their mother. I pray such bonds would exist among my grandchildren, also. That will truly be beautiful, too.

When the weekend was over, they bid each other good-byes and well wishes. They had proudly completed their plan, and I was extremely happy and grateful. They had painted and trimmed my home in its entirety. It really looked good. I was proud that my sons had gladly done the job. Brian went back to Dallas while Garland and his family returned to Huntsville and his work at TDC. Brian's circumstances were less favorable, the drug scene and culture waited for him with greater intensity. Garland's job was spiraling upwards. He was now assigned special duties with the Operation Kick-It program while he was preparing for higher positions. He took inmates to visit schools, organizations, juvenile programs, and community programs. He and the inmates talked to youths to help deter crime. They shared with youth and adult audiences what life is like in a prison. The inmates spoke of their criminal acts and the consequences they suffered for their wrong doings. I could tell he enjoyed being an anti-crime advocate. Garland's inner being was searching to find the right way to help children say "NO" to drugs and crime. He wanted to deter young people from making the same mistakes as his brother. His brother's bad decisions made Garland more dedicated to tell and sell an anti-drug and anti-crime program. He talked with Brian as often as he could and offered him caution about the results and consequences of poor decisions.

When Brian called home, I would call Garland for a three-way conversation. I was still nurturing the bond between these loving brothers. I often laid the phone down and let them enjoy their private conversation which was intensifying their bond. One may wonder how they could continue to bond when their choices of lifestyles continued to be so different. The truth is one brother, Garland, was constantly keeping his brother, Brian, from total self-destruction. Garland continually lifts his brother in prayer. Brian personally feels his brother's love is too important to betray.

Brian desires never to bring shame upon his family members and friends who have helped to keep him within the arch of God's safety. He knows that bonds hold the ropes, not strings, on which he holds for life. He respects his brother and my image by refusing to live in Temple. I have consistently told Brian, "Your being healed of a desire for drugs is more important than any reputation." His love for his family will not allow him to bring discredit upon us intentionally. From their mother's point of view, such personal sacrifice rips my heart out. I want a healed son more than what he perceives as a sterling reputation. I did my best and gave my three children good, honest, and clean foundations on which to build their lives. However, I do not take guilt trips for my adult children's shortcomings. I remain supportive in the healing process of any of their pains.

More importantly, from their mother's point of view, my image will never keep me from standing in the gap when I am needed, despite any differences in their life choices.

20

Brian's Been Shot, He'll Survive

Momma, Brian's Been Shot

Early one morning LaTrell called me from Dallas and said, "Momma, Brian's been shot and is in Baylor University Medical Center." My heart crumbled and I quickly made the right conscious decisions. I called my office and advised my supervisor and staff that I was leaving for Dallas with no certain date of return. I called and told Garland. Easily and quickly I could tell, he was crying. He felt so much pain that I could feel it through the telephone. I told him not to come to Dallas until I visited Brian and gave him an update of Brian's condition. I had no way of knowing Garland previously had a spiritual vision of Brian being in trouble and that he may see him alive for the last time. Garland immediately said, "I will pray for my brother."

I made the most awesome drive to Dallas that I have ever experienced in my life. When I saw the hospital in the skyline, I began to get chills. I decreased my speed as I feared what I might see in my son's desperate hope for life. Parking was scarce but it gave me time to prepare to see my son in the intensive care unit. Tearfully I walked across the parking lot and into the huge lobby. The elevator seemed to take forever and when the doors opened and I stepped in, it felt like a cage that I wanted to burst out of it, to see or not see my ailing son. There was a major part of me that did not want to see him helpless and delirious. That dreadful elevator finally stopped and the door opened. I was scared to walk out into the corridor, but I did. I told the ICU staff whom I wanted to see, and they showed me to my nearly lifeless son. I cannot explain nor know how I felt. Magically, I was empty. His lean body lay in a bed of ice packs, and he had no awareness of my being near. I felt like vanishing. I knew I had to hang on. God had not brought me this far with my children to leave me. I regained composure and went to his bedside as often as I could and as the doctors wanted to update me on his condition.

In the dusk of the evening, I called Garland and told him of this horrible random shooting. I could not, easily, describe in detail Brian's condition; it hurt me too badly. It was very hard for me to see and describe Brian's condition. It was hard but I told Garland, "Your brother has been shot in the trachea at close range. He is in the ICU, and the doctors said they cannot control his infection and fever." It was hard but it was a job that only I could do. I called Brian's father, Mr. Right Soldier Retired, in Tampa, Florida. I knew if Brian's condition became worse, I could not have lived with denying his father the right to know his condition. Mr. Right Soldier Retired said that he would come to visit Brian. Garland called daily for an update on his brother's state of health. I stayed in Dallas all of his hospital stay. Oddly, sleeping in the family waiting room was no problem.

LaTrell was living in Dallas, and she came back and forth to see her brother and to help comfort me. When she went to see him, she wept and spoke softly to his motionless body. She offered her apartment for me to clean myself, rest, and return to the hospital. She gave the same privilege to Mr. Right Soldier Retired when he arrived from Florida. She truly did her part to help her healing brother. One weekend Garland and his wife, Kay, and Kenneth Cannon and his wife, Vanessa, came to see Brian. The sight of Garland's face brought smiling tears to Brian's face and heart. In his faint consciousness, he had a smile for his brother. Garland would kiss him on his forehead and rub him tenderly. When Garland was out of Brian's sight, he wept for his brother's pain and suffering. Garland and Kenneth comforted each other. Kenneth's hug with Garland showed me their bond extended to cherished friendships, too. Kenneth stood by Brian's bedside and whispered sweet words of friendship in his ear. Kenneth's voice caught Brian's subconscious attention. When Brian's eyes opened and saw Kenneth, his eyes were full of smiles as they flashed and danced to let Kenneth know that Catdaddy would fight and survive this ordeal.

When he acknowledged knowing Kenneth was there, Kenneth beamed and said, "Ms. Captain, Catdaddy is going to be okay." Garland and Kenneth's wives watched and prayed. They were witnessing a rarity, black men prayerfully nurturing another black man who is very important to each of them, a brother to one and a very special friend to the other. What a blessing. Kenneth is a very special lifetime friend. Once I visited Brian and Kenneth's shared apartment in Dallas and we "hung out" all day together. I was driving Garland's little standard shift Opal. We went to many shopping malls. We ate out, played like children, and enjoyed a whole day as mother and sons. Kenneth affectionately calls Brian, "Catdaddy."

From their mother's point of view, I don't know what

Catdaddy means, but it was important enough for Kenneth and his wife to stay overnight in Dallas in order to be with his friend in this time of need. I thanked God for my children's ability to make and keep good friendships. A good friend is worth more than silver and gold. Kenneth and Vanessa are worth more than their weight in gold.

Garland spoke with the physicians to be certain of his brother's condition. When he visited Brian's bedside, it was terribly painful for me to see their shared pain. There lay Brian in a bed with wooden splints that spread his legs and arms and fixed his head and neck. The bed oscillated like the motion of a swinging hammock. The doctors wanted his body to move but not for him to move himself; his spinal cord was too fragile. His body lay in a bed of ice packs, covered only by a loin cloth and one sheet. We asked the physicians question after question; they were patient and answered all of our questions. The surgeries to remove the bullet were for naught; it is still lodged in his body, somewhere. Infection could not be controlled, and success in the repaired trachea was unknown because it had not been tested. Fever and more fever was uncontrollable. Consequently, he was frequently delirious. He had enough blood transfusions to fill three bodies. The infection continued to contaminate the new blood.

Prayers and more prayers were said by Garland, Kenneth, and me. We rubbed his body, kissed his face and hands, and continued to pray. Many friends and relatives prayed with us and for him. His faint consciousness gave us smiles of confidence in our dedication to his well-being. Brian's father came from Tampa, Florida. He seemed to truly care, but he seemed surprised by the prayers, love, and bonding that was shown for Brian's recovery. As the weekend was closing, Garland called the family together, including Kenneth and Vanessa and Mr. Right Soldier

Retired. He had us form a prayer circle and he prayed. Mr. Right Soldier Retired seemed astonished by the prayer circle. He also seemed uncertain about Garland's giving him a holy hug. He seemed to not relate to the depth of these brothers' love. He never had a brother, hence he knew nothing about brotherly love. He could not relate to the bond between these brothers.

Mr. Right Soldier Retired again was unkind to me. As I wept for Brian's healing and kissed his face, Mr. Right Solder Retired damned me for kissing Brian. He said I was putting germs on him. I resented and ignored his stupidity. Since I knew he did not know much about love, I ignored him and kissed my son anyway. The doctors had told me that my presence helped his healing. They said that he smiled when they referred to me and I made a positive difference in his improvement. As his mother, I did not need anyone to sanction my relationship with my son. We love each other too much to let anyone bring us grief, including Mr. Right Soldier Retired.

During my stay in the ICU family waiting room, I received two annoying telephone calls. One was from a friend who asked "Myrt, did he get shot over some drugs?" I told her, "I don't know." She said, "That's all I wanted to know" and closed our conversation. She did not offer one word of comfort nor concern. Another lady called and told me, "The Lord told me to call and caution you to not hate the person who shot Brian." I was stunned.

She said, "When my son was in that car wreck, I learned that I loved him more than I did God." I was angered and told her, "I have never loved my children more than God, because He gave them to me." I told her, "This is not the first time I have faced God over a hospital bed of my sick children. I met Him when Garland was a very small boy and he received emergency surgery on his arm." I told her, "I met Him when LaTrell, as an adult was in a nasty and deadly car wreck, I held her unconscious in my arms. Again, I met him when LaTrell had an emergency gall bladder surgery." I thought about when I had been a victim of several nasty car wrecks in which I had many broken bones, requiring surgery in my face. I told her, "Thanks for the call, but God had never gotten a busy signal when he called me nor when he notified me of Brian's tragedy."

From their mother's point of view, God called and came to see us in our many and darkest hours of despair, pain, suffering, and confusion. He didn't ask if it was drugs and hang up. I was like the lady with the issue of blood. He felt me tugging on his heart and took care of me en route to my son's bedside. Each time God called or came, He stayed with each of us until we were comforted. As for His phone calls, God has never missed me when He called me. I have never gotten a busy signal when I called Him. I don't doubt the Lord spoke to her, but I knew He knows my number, too. As for the friend who simply wanted to know if it was about drugs, I dismissed her call. I know misery loves company.

After the doctors were satisfied that he was healing and the trachea was out of danger, the next prognosis was equally as terrifying. The physicians told me the esophagus and trachea are so close that they feared the esophagus might be damaged, too. They said if the esophagus had a tiny hole, he would not survive and the struggle to save his life would be for naught. This experience taught me the esophagus is the one part of the body that doctors have not learned to repair nor replace. The physicians told us only when they begin to pour fluid in him could they tell if the esophagus had a leak. We went into prayer again. Garland's response was, "I know God has not brought us this far to leave us." We prayed fervently. The doctors were pleased to tell us despite the microscopic space between the repaired trachea and the esophagus, there was no damage to the esophagus and he would not have to wear the commonly known device called a voice box. Jubilance and praise for God's mercy rang through our hearts. Garland thanked God for sparing his brother's life. I thanked God for the whole experience, for within everything God allows, there is a blessing. This experienced taught me there are no more blessed words than, "Your son is out of danger."

From their mother's point of view, there is no greater love than the love a man has for his healing brother. Also, from one brother to the other, they demonstrated their love for each other.

Brian's Weeks of Recovery

After more than six weeks in ICU, he was recovered. After many visits and many sleepless nights, I felt relieved when the doctors said I could take him home. I sang praises to God for the many days He hovered over Brian's death's door. I asked Keith to go with me to bring his dad home. Keith was happy to help me to bring Brian home from the hospital. Keith pushed the wheelchair and did everything to comfort his dad. I drove us home and placed him in the middle bedroom, which was his sister's bedroom when they were children and next to my bedroom so I could easily hear his needs. I had recently redecorated the bedroom in cool colors of pastel blue, gray, and white. He said that the room made him at ease and peaceful like a healing prince. It was a joy to cook for him, care for him, and nurture him to good health. When he called, I rushed and answered with pleasure. I could not help but recall how I prayed in the ICU for him to just see my face and know I was near. I learned how to lift him from and lay him in the bed without horrible pain. That was difficult. When the telephone rang and I said, "It's your brother," he would smile and get happy. While they talked his face kept a smile. And I left the room. I knew they had a bond that only they shared in the depths of their hearts. I owed them private conversations. I knew when they were closing a conversation, Brian would say, "I love you, too." Garland closes all of our telephone conversations with "I love—my momma." I could guess he had said "I love you" or "I love my brother." Garland holds such great esteem for his brother. He still calls Brian "my big brother," despite his towering height of 6'4" and holding a firm 245 pounds of imposing stature. Brian is 6' and weighs about 165. Brian is the little big brother, and Garland is the big little brother. Yet, Brian still says, "When I grow up, I want to be like my little brother." They make my heart smile when they make these expressions of respect and love for each other.

From their mother's point of view, it's okay for my sons to hold a revered place in each other's hearts that I have no right to enter. Bonding is all about having a special love for a special person. Bonding also means being able to do and be all that someone needs when they need it. Both of them hold a special place for me, too.

Brian's Checkup and Progress

I took Brian to and from the Baylor University Medical Center, in Dallas, for checkups. When the physicians asked how his ribs were healing, we were surprised. We did not know the doctors had broken his ribs in order to open his chest cavity to perform the required surgery. We smiled as we realized why he had so much pain when I helped him into and from the bed.

From their mother's point of view, helping to restore the life of my little eaglet was a powerful and rewarding experience. It is something I wish would never have happened, but I am glad I was there for him and was able to provide the help and loving care that he needed. I knew Garland was happy that I was able to give Brian daily tender loving care. I know I had no control over these circumstances, but I did have control over my response. Love and care were his better medicines, and I had plenty of each. One of his antibiotics cost me over $98 per prescription refill. The whole ordeal was extremely costly, but it was a joy for me to help mend the broken wing of my little eaglet and to enhance his healing process.

Garland and I Go into Prayer

Garland and I told Brian, "We have prayed for your body and mind to no longer hunger for drugs and the fast life of Dallas." We knew that he loved Dallas. It seemed Brian could not resist the yearning to return and live in Dallas. Brian said Dallas had more employment opportunities than Temple. He was right. There is still very little employment opportunities in Temple, Texas for young black men to make enough wages to enjoy a few of life's pleasures and provide for their families to live comfortably.

From their mother's point of view, it hurts to know the city that we live in and love does not take care of its black youth as it does many others. Most of our children must move to other cities to earn a decent salary. Those who stay here are more often subject to becoming involved in criminal activities, joining the vicious cycle of underemployed, and entering and reentering prison. It is the twisted fate of life's vicious cycle of either poverty or imprisonment. A small number have achieved success at home.

Brian's Desire to Return to Dallas

Brian's healing process was in my sheltered environment. I spent time thinking about and thanking God for my career being intact and secure enough for my absence from work. Taking time off my job had no adverse affect on my employment. I did a lot of my work by telephone. God was not mad at me. I think He was proud of me for taking care of the eaglet he entrusted to me on May 17, 1960. Garland's career in the Texas Department of Corrections (TDC) was taking off like a jet. Brian's desire to return to Dallas had to be honored. It broke my heart when he returned to Dallas, what I call the pits of hell. In Dallas, unemployed young black males are fresh and tender meat for the vicious beasts of the drug world. Garland and I prayed daily that he would be led in the right direction and his health would be protected. We know that prayers left with God will be answered in His time and in His way. I struggled with accepting that reality.

From their mother's point of view, I took our burdens to the Lord and left them there. Though I left them with God, I feared for his freedom, safety, and health. I accepted the fact that I can not solve all of my children's problems. I also know that God does not hold me responsible for my adult children's shortcomings. Garland and I knew we had no right to make Brian's decisions. I don't have the right to dictate to my adult children what they should do with their lives. When my little eaglet was healed and ready to fly again, he flew to Dallas. Painfully, I stood and watched him fly away.

21

Overwhelming Dallas

Brian's Stay in Dallas

Brian rented a room from an elderly lady. She had a lot of attributes like my mother. Brian loved her and related to her as he did my mother. Soon it was evident the other fellows who roomed with her were serious drug users. This was truly the pits of hell and renewed his hunger for drugs, which led to several trips to Dallas County jail. He was given probation and released back to the same deadly streets of Dallas. I learned that when judges get tired of seeing the same persons again and again, they slam-dunk drug offenders. All I could do was pray, the best thing for Brian's future.

While in the Dallas County jail, Brian called me weeping and said, "Momma, you can lessen the likelihood of my being sent to prison." I listened. He asked, "Please write a letter to the judge and state my case. Please ask him to get me into a SAF P program rather than prison."

I wrote the best letter that I could. My worldly conscious suggested that I not write the letter and let him go to prison with no afterthought. Quickly, I shook that insanity out of my mind. I recalled doing so much more for other young people in trouble. I knew I had to give my very best effort to save my own son; tears dropped from my eyes as I pounded the keys on my computer keyboard. I felt God's presence and guidance as my fingers danced across the keys of my keyboard. They were whipping out words of a compassionate plea that startled me as I read them from my computer screen. I tried to understand that if a young man uses drugs, he is taking his own life. If he goes to prison for using drugs, the system is also taking his life. It seemed his life was being taken twice. I soon learned how this vicious circle saw of life works; it bites coming and going. I learned the cruel drug-infested world seeks our children and takes them from us, from themselves, and from a free society.

The most frightening thing that happened, during that time, was when Isaac, the third foreign exchange student I housed, and I visited a prison unit with Garland. I saw what appeared to me to be a garbage disposal of humanity. I saw young and old men who appeared happy while being incarcerated. I saw faces of young and old men who were institutionalized and seemed to be at home, in the prison. I saw faces of young and old men who seemed not to care about the loss of their freedom. My heart silently cried out, "Lord, please don't let my Brian lose sight of the many good things I have taught him and the beauty of his freedom. Lord, please don't let my son become an institutionalized prisoner." My heart screamed out, "Lord, please show me what, and how, I can help Brian turn his life around." Garland remained vigilant in his prayers for Brian. Garland also prayed for a revelation on how he could help his brother turn himself around.

From their mother's point of view, Garland exhibited love that went beyond my teaching. Their brotherly love transcends all of my ability to teach nor understand. Their love is God-driven. I need only to not interfere.

Brian Goes to Court

Brian's day in court came. My brother rode to Dallas with me. Brian had to face an awesome hard-core judge. Brian's court appointed attorney said to me, "I hate you had to come so far, but the judge is not in a good mood today. He is sending everybody down (to prison) for a long time." He continued, "Brian is not a person who needs to be in prison; he just needs help to kick this awful addiction." I agreed. The attorney asked me to please let him put it off until another day. My first thought was, this was an unnecessary trip. However, my faith and trust in God told me, **PEACE, BE STILL** and to be patient. If there was any chance to preclude Brian's being sent to prison, it was not a wasted trip. It turned out to be a blessed trip. A week later he was placed on the docket to come before the same judge, again. I was praying that my letter had softened his heart and he would show Brian some compassion.

When the officers escorted Brian into the courtroom in shackles and white overalls, my heart sank. I too, approached the bench. The judge asked me if I wanted to say something. I said, "Yes, sir." He sternly said to me, "Don't talk to me, talk to your son; you've done nothing to be here in front of me." Brian's facial expression and a muffled voice agreed with the judge and said, "You are right, sir, she has done nothing to cause this. I did."

Those words pierced my heart, deeply. Unfortunately, I was ill and full of cold, fever, and not feeling well at all, but I had to stand in the gap for my son, again. I was afraid the judge might think I was seeking a pity party with my frail voice. With the best voice I could muster, I spoke to Brian. Seemingly, God stepped into the chambers of my heart and dictated what I should say to my son before this awesome judge.

I told my son, "I hope the judge can see you are not bad nor have you been a bad person." I continued, "My heart is bleeding for your predicament. I know you would rather not be hooked on such an evil vice as drugs." I told him, ". . . No matter where you will be, I will love you as long as I live." Additionally, I said, " I pray the judge will send you to a SAF P program and give you an opportunity in a controlled environment dedicated to the cure of addictions and be healed."

My son stood like a man, with tears of regret for my pain, rolling down his cheeks. Though his eyes never blinked, the tears were rolling down both of his cheeks. We both noticed the whole court room had come to absolute silence. He faced the judge and took the consequences for his actions, like a man. There were many people in the court room for their own problems, yet, they had quieted and were intently listening to my pleas for my first son. I felt so defenseless and weak. The tears on my son's cheeks looked as if they needed me to kiss and rub them away. But they would not allow me to touch him. Silently, my heart cried out again, "Lord, I just want to touch him."

My heart begged and asked, why did I have to pay such a price? I could not think of an answer. I just wanted to touch him. My mental tapes made a replay to the day when he was less than four years old and told me, "Momma, it can't be that bad." At that precise moment, I knew it was worse than the day when he soothed my aching wounds. I stood tall and erect while my total inner being was crumbling into many small pieces. What a painful feeling it was to see my son crying and I could not touch him. When I finished my three minutes of talking to my son, my body felt weak as if I had instantly lost thirty pounds. Brian turned to the judge for his decision. The judge said, "Mr. Flakes, I believe you have been a bad son and one your mother does not deserve." Brian agreed and told him, "I have been a bad son, and she does not deserve having to be here." My heart sank deeper. The judge made some scathing comments to Brian. His voice sound so callous, cold, heartless, and bitter. I knew the judge meant to drive home a strong commitment from Brian to become a part of his own solution or otherwise he would continue to be the author of his problems. I stood lifeless as this awesome judge scolded my first son. Brian stood erect and took it like a man. He agreed with the judge. "It is time for me to make a serious change in my life and lifestyle." He pleaded for help. "I know I need help. But, the problem is too big and bad for me to do it alone. I want to rid myself of this sick addiction."

The judge told him, "Mr. Flakes, you have to want to do it for yourself. I once smoked more than three packs of cigarettes per day and I was only hurting me. I had to decided to stop smoking for my own health and I did." After more words of caution, the judge remanded him to Dallas County Jail, pending being sent to a SAF P program. I had learned the SAF P program would place him in a safe environment for real healing, teaching, restoration of worthiness, and self-discipline. Softly and pleadingly I whispered to the judge, "May I hug him?" The judge's face softened, and he softly said, "No, it's against the rules."

Again my heart sank deeper. Brian was ushered away from me. From his back I saw the shackles on his feet and hands. I felt like screaming, I thought he looked like a prison inmate, but I knew I could not scream. It was a sight that actually snatched a huge hunk out of my total existence. I tried to collect my thoughts, in a hurry. I could not. I wanted to race out of the court room. I could not. I wanted to scream, "Thank you, Lord, for SAF P over the dungeons of despair," the unit I had seen while visiting the prison with my baby son. It seemed like miles from the judge's bench to the first observer's seat.

I sat in the observers' seat to rest. I was tired and drained. I felt a need for more than a gallon of water. My brother said, "Well, he took him away from you." I did not try to process his statement, I knew he was proud because my son was in jail as he had been for so many times. He seemed to relish his going to a penitentiary. I simply told him, "No, he just gave him back to me." My brother did not immediately understand my rationale and asked, "What do you mean?"

I just sat there motionless and tried to think. I could only think that the judge gave my son a chance to truly get some healing. I had learned Brian's being on the streets of Dallas was like a sheep in a den of hungry wolves. I knew the reality of my son's addiction made him too weak to resist the temptations of the drug world. I also felt relief in knowing for a period of time that I would know his whereabouts and that his well-being would be safe. I told my brother I could see myself watching the 10:00 P.M. news and when they say, "It is ten o'clock; do you know where your children are?" I can say, "Yes, my Brian is in a safe place of recovery." The walk from the court room to the elevator and to the first floor and onto my car in the parking lot seemed to be miles and miles. I was sick, tired, troubled, and sad.

From their mother's point of view, both of my sons are so precious to me and while I was trying to save one, the other one was praying for his brother to be saved. There is a relief in knowing that Garland never gave up on Brian and he never will. My sons love each other, uncompromisingly. There is a relief in knowing their love cannot be threatened nor tainted by anything at any time. I continuously thank God for standing in the gap with me.

A Quiet and Lonely Ride Home

With my brother, I drove from Dallas with an empty heart and physically drained. I was speechless. Physically, I was beginning to feel worse, my head was clogged, I felt feverish and drowsy. I felt as if I was beginning to have the flu. I visited my mother at the nursing center and told her of Brian's being sent to a prison setting. She said, "I am partly responsible for that too, ain't I?" I could only say "Yes." I guess she was thinking about how many times she had betrayed my judgment with my son and having told me "I have a bad son; there's nothing wrong with you having one too."

Each time she told me that, I always felt nothing but contempt for her. I could not understand how my mother could wish her first grandson to be a bad son. I could not understand her wishing her only daughter's son being a bad son. I prayed hard for an understanding. I still cannot understand her idiocy. Her mean-spirited mentality toward me and my children shredded my heart and totally consumed my being. I felt I had to struggle daily to keep my son from being a bad son, like her son. I felt she wanted my son to go to prison as did her son, many times, for many different things done to himself and others. Each time my Brian had a problem, I could hear her mean-spirited laughter and repetition of her thoughts that I should have a bad son, too.

I spent many sleepless nights crying because she always betrayed and humiliated my better judgment and encouraged Brian and LaTrell to "have fun." Repeatedly, I told her the term "have fun" in today's sick society means death to our youth. She laughed. In my heart I knew it was not okay for me to have a bad child. It was not okay, because I had carefully and deliberately structured my children's home life to avoid the temptations of wild and dangerous living that my brother and I were exposed to through the traffic of riotous roomers. I worked hard and sacrificed to afford for my children the best of things to make their lives happy, healthy, wholesome, clean, and risk free. I monitored their behavior and corrected any misbehavior on the spot. I never failed to tell them how much I loved them, something she never did for me. I knew all the right things that I did for of my children meant I deserved good children and they deserved the best life has to offer. My mother's interference made a difference in my children's response to my upbringing. It was painful to lose either of my children. I resented her making deliberate efforts to make Brian be impressed with becoming a bad son. I still cannot understand nor appreciate her driving a huge wedge between my brother and me, between my daughter and me, and between my first son and me.

She could not take nor buy Garland's love nor his loyalty from me. My children are the people who should love me too much to hurt me. Today, I can only believe she truly never wanted me, nor cared for, nor loved me. How else could she bring me so much pain? My children and I are still living, and therefore healing and mending can take place. There remains one thing I love but don't understand: "Why is it that only Garland could see the wrath my mother repeatedly showered on me?" It must be the fact that I made the right choice and gave him his right to birth. He has truly been the blessing God knew I needed.

Garland has been a pillar and support in all of my trying times. His love and care for me has not been shaken by anyone, and I feel confident no one can take his love for his mother from me. I know no one can take nor shake my love for him. This does not mean that I love my other two children less. It is only an acknowledgment of Garland's and my love for love each other. My mother has passed away, but many awesome and painful memories of her linger but are not as piercing. Brian was confined in Dallas County Jail and was not able to attend her funeral. That hurt him deeply, and I grieved for his absence. He told me that he could not come to his grandmother's funeral escorted and shackled. He said, "I love her too much to bring such embarrassment to her funeral service."

Little Brittany has grown a lot but still has a way of soothing my wounds. Naturally, she knows what I need and when. She always shows up on time. During my hours of bereavement for my mother and regret for Brian's absence, Brittany sweetly nestled close to me and said, "I hope Uncle Brian will be able to come to my high school graduation." I think she knew my unhappiness was largely because of Brian's absence. I could only say, "I am sure he will be there, baby," and I hugged her tightly.

When I told Brian of Brittany's request, he remembered her saying that she wanted to live next door to her Uncle Brian. He looked straight at me and said, "Momma, she is giving me plenty of notice, six years. I won't let her down." Brian understood that she probably had an idea of where he was, but that did not make her love him less. How could this happen? She has a daddy who lets it be known that he loves his brother. She is wise like her daddy and will say nothing to make someone unhappy. Her sweet statement of her uncle and during my bereavement of my mother made my heart happy. I think she knew I wished for Brian's presence and a chance for him to attend his grandmother's funeral.

I have given serious thought to our present situation. For the first time in my children's life, I would have them without Ruby's negative influence and interference. Maybe, the sting of my mother's negative interference will vanish from my memories. If it doesn't vanish, I know for sure they cannot be repeated. Thanks, Brittany, for your wisdom and timing. Your sweet gesture to your suffering grandmother surpassed your years of age. Now I am blessed with a wise granddaughter to help soothe my aching heart.

From my point of view, her death and arranging the funeral service was difficult because I always loved my mother despite the pain she caused. As I thought of my sons, one confined and one managing a confinement facility, their hearts were joined at their grandmothers funeral. I felt it was beautiful to see a brother let it be known, in trying times, that he loves his brother. This point of view is for either or both. Their love and support are mutual. An additional point of view: it has to be love that keeps Brian's esteem for his brother, while he remains responsible for his own actions.

Brian has never accused me of preferential treatment among any of my three children. He consistently tells all sociologists and counselors, "My mom is a single mother, but we never missed anything by not having a father in the house." He tells me, ". . . Momma, you are not to be blamed for my choices. You taught and showed me the right things to do." Very recently, Brian told Garland, "I am just realizing, man, what a powerful mother we have. Good thing there was no father; he probably would have messed it all up." They agreed and laughed together.

That helps to soothe some of my longtime heartaches and pains. I encourage young single parents to realize they are in charge of both the *yes* and the *no*. I urge them to not abuse that power and to diligently seek God's guidance. I am proof that He will see us through. I often hear young single mothers say "I can do bad by myself," I verbally chastise them and say, ". . . Don't ever let me hear you say that again; **you can do good by yourself.**"

22
SAF P

Brian's Stay in SAF P

I visited Brian in the SAF P, Breckenridge, Texas facility, once every four to five weeks. He was assigned to the Breckenridge Facility from November 1996 to August of 1997. With each trip the four-hour drive became easier. At the SAF P, I could hug and kiss him when I arrived and left. I wanted to hug him more, but the two hugs were better than when the judge told me not to touch him. I learned from Garland how to stand on a solid rock and to provide for my sons the strong motherly support through this rough, tough, trying and growing time in Brian's life. I leaned on and trusted God and Garland's wisdom over mine. Garland sees, knows, and works with drug offenders daily. He understands how some of the offenders get to TDC. He has learned what it takes to help restore worthiness in men who have not reassessed their value and learned how to move forward from that juncture in their lives.

During each of my visits, Brian and I talked deeply, mended a lot of fences, and rewired some communication disconnections. Through Garland's advice, I could see some real healing and self-actualization taking place in

Brian's mind. I could tell that drugs had not burned his brain. Garland wrote to Brian regularly and sent him pictures of himself and his family. Brian told me that he did not want the people at his unit to know his baby brother was a warden. He said he did not want to shame his brother. Yet, Garland told me that he did not visit Brian at the SAF P because often offenders mistreat each other if they learn an offender has a relative in a meaningful position within TDC. He did not want Brian to endure any unnecessary harassment. I felt blessed that both of my son's valued each other's character and safety in such trying times.

For Brian's thirty-seventh birthday, Garland sent him $37.37. Brian thought that was such a sweet gesture. Garland told his staff that his brother was in a SAF P similar to the one for which he serves as the Senior Warden. He told them his brother's case helps to serve as a reason that he expects to help heal the men in his unit and to help them to make meaningful changes in their lives for their futures. Painted on a sign at the entrance and major hall wall in his unit is his motto for the unit: "Changing Lives—Making a Difference."

From their mother's point of view, these two brothers are the epitome of excellent role models for what can happen even in the best of families. They represent what constant nurturing and love can do to maintain a healthy and loving bond, no matter the problems. They show how a mother can hold the strings of hope when things get rough. They show how "doing the right thing" can have so many different positive meanings. They show how each one can step in and help when either needs the other. I love knowing that I can still say, "Boys, come here," and they want to come together. Oh, how happy that makes my heart.

My Visit to Uganda, East Central Africa

I took a month long trip to Uganda, East Central Africa, while Brian was in the SAF P. However, I made sure he got mail from me each alternate day. A friend mailed cards to Brian for me. She made sure that he got mail at mail call. He laughed and said, "What is going on? I get mail from my mother from Temple and the next day from Africa." Brian had taught me how important it was to receive mail at mail call. It boosted his self-esteem. He said all the men must report for mail call and those who never got mail always felt disappointed, embarrassed, and sad because they felt rejected by their family and friends each time there was "no mail" at mail call. I thought it must be hard to be confined and rejected, too. I could tell by Brian's letters that he was truly feeling a positive change in his outlook at life and that he desired some positive changes in his life. He helped me to deal with many of the things that made my heart ache. We talked deeply and he explained how drug addiction can creep upon a person when he thinks it is just a social usage. He had someone in the unit to do art on the envelopes in which he mailed my letters. He knows that I love eagles. One envelope had two eagles. It was a mother eagle protecting her eaglet. Another one had a picture of my 1963 classic and snazzy little red Ford Falcon Futura convertible. One had hearts chained together through the jail bars; it was so powerful that it is used for the cover of this book. It shows us—Brian, Garland, and me—through the jail bars as we remained linked together; our hearts were indeed connecting. In this case that it represents Brian and Garland, the links in the chain read, "Mom." The beauty of this art is that the one on the outside or inside of the bars could be either one of us. None of us rejected Brian because of his confinement. None of us deserted him in his deepest hour of need. One letter had a long-stem red rose penciled in the middle of his stationary.

All of these things were gestures of growth and humble expressions of love and a serious plea for forgiveness. He never had a habit of lying to me; therefore, I believe he was telling me the truth about coming to a new level of understanding of what he has to do for himself in order to live the life that he deserves. He said that he realizes that I never had specific high, nor demanding expectations for either of them, but I always had high hopes for all three of them. He went further to say, "You provided us all the tools necessary for achieving high hopes and aspirations." That is one of the most profound compliments that he could have given me. I know he is absolutely right. I never dictated to either of my children what they must do or be. I certainly taught them to be the best of whatever they chose. Repeatedly I showed them support to help them accomplish anything they needed and wanted to become.

From their mother's point of view, it is a beautiful morning in life when adult children are able to find the route in life that leads them to success. It is a beautiful morning, when forgiveness exists between family members. It is a beautiful morning when members of a family can honestly say, "I love you and am willing to show and do whatever is needed to receive love in return." Love is not an automatic genetic makeup. Love has to come from within, and it grows when the recipients give love in return. I have also come to know that a beautiful morning does not always come at 6:00 A.M. It comes anytime we open our minds, eyes, and/or hearts and let the joy of being loved move inside our own being. Prior to such an experience, the relationship is in the dark. Joy does come in the morning. I have learned that love and hate does not dwell in the same temple. We generally accept the term, "I love you, but I hate what you do." That can be true, but if we continue to hate what one does, we begin to think what one does is synonymous with the total person. This is not to say that we should love murdering because a family may be a vicious murderer. It makes us know that we are not responsible for the actions of others, and therefore we can still love the member who does unacceptable things against themselves and or society.

It Is Time for Brian to Be Released

Soon it seemed that August was upon us and Brian's release date was near. Brian sent me the official request for release clothing. Garland gave me fifty dollars and helped me to select, buy, and mail to Brian the things that he needed for release. We carefully selected good colors to match the quality of things that we know he appreciates. We chose a button-collar shirt because he does not like his surgery scar in his throat and chest to show. We chose soft shoes because his feet are fragile. I chose a genuine leather belt because he loves wearing belts and nice quality pants. We were pleased when he received the box that we mailed because he was very happy about our choices. We knew he would be grateful because he is a naturally appreciative person. Brian told me, "Momma, you and Garland have saved me again." He told me there were several young men with nothing to wear when leaving the SAF P program. I asked, "What did they do?" He said, "They were given some Goodwill or Salvation Army clothing." I felt bad for the other young men's lacking. I thanked God that Garland and I sent him release clothing and had supported him during his stay in the SAF P.

He expressed his gratefulness for the items and for our selections.

From their mother's point of view, I know and regret that drugs made some dark days in Brian's life. I know that Brian's knowing his brother loved and supported his recovery helped to make his days brighter and more hopeful. Our positive reinforcement had a lot to do with his getting through the maze of that experience. The whole saga was and still is God's business, and He will deliver us more joy with each coming morning.

My Baby's Wise Counsel

Garland told me, "Usually men begin to turn around when they are in their middle thirties." I learn to believe him, and he encouraged me to have faith and be of good courage. He believed that Brian would experience total recovery and become a strong person capable of maximizing his potentials and give back to society.

Garland has worked through TDC from a Correctional Officer to becoming a senior warden of the Richard P. LeBlanc Substance Abuse Facility with 1,000 beds and approximately 300 employees under his supervision, before the age of 34. He has some options to offer Brian for his consideration for his future. However, he and I recognize that we cannot dictate where, nor how, Brian must live his life. It has to be his exclusive decision. I will never think their bond happened only because I loved my children, but I can say that I have always been there for each of them when they needed me. I cannot say that I did everything right in my parenting these three lovely young people, but I can say I never intentionally did anything to harm them. I cannot say there have never been any childish pranks, mischief, or arguments between them, but I can say they have always loved each other, no matter when or what were their needs. I can say my intentional teaching and nurturing my three children did not hurt them. I may not have responded in some ways totally as they wanted, but I did do what my best wisdom dictated at the time.

From their mother's point of view, I can say their bond is more than I envisioned. I thank God for His divine intervention when I was not wise nor smart enough to meet our needs.

Bonds Create Respect for Each Other

During plans for a Christmas dinner, both Brian and Garland planned and were home at the same time. Often, work and life prevented that from occurring. When they arrived they greeted each other with a hug and a holy kiss. I smiled and enjoyed each second of their relationship as brothers. They grow stronger toward each other with time and age. We moved to the dining room table. Garland sat in a side chair. Brian told him, "You sit in the head chair with the arms." I just sat and watched. Garland knew Brian was thinking he (Brian) had not been the ideal son to merit the armed chair. Garland responded, "No, you are always going to be my big brother." I just sat and watched. Brian stood beside the armed chair, held it out for Garland, and told him, "You have earned it." My heart sank and vocal cords silently squalled out, "God, I thank you." Yet, I just sat there and watched.

Brian stood beside the armed chair and with his certain look, he gave Garland the clear message to sit in the armed chair. Brian stood there and held the armed chair out until Garland moved to the armed chair. Brian assisted him, by pushing it under the table and then he sat in a side chair. I just sat there and watched. There was nothing in the world that could be powerful enough to say or do that would add any more evidence of their being bonded and respectful of each other. I think Brian's being the oldest makes Garland respect his being the senior. Regardless of the life choices they have made, Brian knew that Garland has listened and stayed focused on their home training, and to him that made Garland worthy of the armed chair. From their mother's point of view, what more could I ask for than to see my two sons deal with each other like real men? I know their love for each other has not been tarnished by time, nor shaken by circumstances, nor thwarted by choices either good or bad. Neither of their love has been nor can be swayed by anyone.

Again, from their mother's point of view, life is worth living when you can die and leave siblings in love with each other. When the death angel comes to give me a ride to heaven, I can leave happily, knowing my children were taught how to love each other. I believe they will never experience sibling rivalry nor abuse because they know I love each of them deeply and individually. They know I want them to always respect and be a comfort and source of strength when either of the others need support.

23

We Lived the Past, See the Future, and We're Moving On

Their Lives Will Always Be Roses

Do I think their lives will be all roses forever? Yes, I do think their lives will forever be roses. However, I don't forget all rose bushes have thorns. Their lives are always going to be beautiful and smell sweet like roses. Yet, just like a rose bush, their lives will have to be lived cautiously, because like life, rose bushes have thorns. I have no doubt their bond and love for each other will always be very important. I have an assurance that one son being a Senior Warden will not lessen his love for his brother who has had an experience in the State of Texas recovery program. I have an assurance their bond has been tested. It has withstood the test of time and people who said anything to us and tried to make us feel ashamed or bad about things that are commonplace in many families. Yes, we feel pain for any of our lost days and months and years of prosperous living. We feel blessed that Brian knows the difference and is remorseful for the pains that he has caused himself and those who love him so deeply. I have grown tremendously by having Garland to keep me on track and not letting anything taint my desire to support those I love no matter the circumstances.

From their mother's point of view, it is okay to learn from my children. I would be foolish if I ignored the wisdom and knowledge these fine young people possess and offer. God has blessed me to live long enough for them to realize that I have dedicated my life to their well-being and will always be a support for any of their problems.

I Don't Have a Bad Son

I hated my mother's saying it was okay for me to have a bad son, as she did. I detested what my brother became and was adamant that I would not have a son like him. For too long I allowed my mother to say that Brian was my bad son and that he and my brother were identical. Garland told me, "Momma, Brian is not a bad son."

I have thought more deeply about the difference between Brian and my brother. Brian never cut a man's nose off and kept the nose in his pocket, as my brother did. Brian never went to prison repeatedly to both federal and state, as my brother did. Brian never hurt his sister nor fought her like he was a mad dog, as my brother fought me. Brian has never treated me like my brother did our mother. Brian never stole from me as my brother did from our mother. Brian never let drunken stupor disturb my sleep all night as my brother did our mother. Brian has never done any of the mean vicious things to other people as did my brother.

I have learned that no matter how wrong a mother can be, we tend to believe whatever she says to us. I hate that I did not rebuke her notion that Brian was my bad son; he is not a bad son. He is a wonderful son who made some bad decisions, and I am so glad that God has allowed me to live long enough to tell my son, "I know you are not a bad son." I have told my son, "Brian, you are not a bad son; you are a beautiful and caring person. You love your family in the way that God would have us to love each other, without conditions."

I have grown to a new level and final decision, which is that I do not have a bad son. I have two good sons. My baby son knew what he wanted when he was a little boy, and he stayed focused until he reached his goals in life. My first son has made some bad decisions and has been blessed by God to have experienced real recovery. He is coming in on the last leg of the race to accept the gold rings of life's race. I have every reason to believe that he will bring the gold trophy home. My son Brian has never been a bad person. I regret that I did not have this revelation sooner; it would have saved both of our hearts some pain. I feel blessed more each day to have a beautiful daughter and two wonderful sons and know that they love each other. I believe my death will bring my children closer, the contrary of my mother's death; it has forced my brother and I to extreme opposite ends of reasoning. It seems that bonding between us will never happen. At this stage of my life I am too fatigued to struggle for bonding or caring. I totally ignore his rude telephone calls and insulting messages he leaves on my answering machine.

Where Do We Go from Here?

Where do we go from here? I don't know exactly. But, I believe in the depths of my heart that nothing in life will ever diminish nor tarnish the love and bond between the warden, his brother, and their sister.

From their mother's point of view, they and their sister represent the best things in life. They have great character, strong courage, integrity, resilience, love and respect for God and each other. They don't have the sibling rivalry that I have lived with for a lifetime. They have sibling love that grows closer and stronger each day. Though the boys have a special bond, they deeply love their beautiful and effervescent sister, Charmin LaTrell.

Did This Book Help Their Mother?

This book and its companion book titled *Twisted Fate* have been a gut-wrenching experience for me. *Twisted Fate* expounds on many of the awesome situations in this book. I have surfaced and disclosed things that were hidden deep in the dark locked basement of my mind. I have allowed myself to express things I buried deep in the crevices of my mind and heart. These two books have caused me to share my own conscious secrets. Some, I hid from myself. I thought some of my secrets were so valuable and awful that it would be devastating for others to know. I have learned those secrets did not need to be secrets, at all. I was told that my retirement from work is the first time I have truly been free. I believe it, too, but from another point of view, real freedom is when I could face me and know that I am free from secrets that have burned and agonized my heart for years. It is comforting to realize there are no secrets so horrendous that I must take them to my grave. Real freedom is being able to look myself straight in the eye and know I don't harbor any ill feelings with nor about me. I am free. A poem that I learned while in my Homemaking class of Dunbar High

School best states how I feel about myself with the burden of secrets being removed from my total being.

Myself

I have to live with myself and so,
I want to be fit for myself to know.
I want to be able as days go by,
Always to look myself, straight in the eye;
I don't want to hide on a closet shelf,
A lot of secrets about myself.
I don't want to stand with the setting sun,
And hate myself for the things I have done,
I want to go out with my head erect,
I want to deserve all men's respect
For here in this struggle for fame and wealth,
I want to be able to like myself.
I don't want to look at myself and know,
That I am a bluster and bluff and empty show.
I can never fool myself and so
Because I know what others may never know
Whatever happens I want to be
Self-respecting and conscience free.

—Author Unknown

In closing this writing, I'd emphasize siblings can and must be taught to love and bond with each other. They can be taught to love and bond even if brick and mortar walls may separate them. They can be taught to love and bond when one sits at the desk across from the other with no regards of what position the other one holds.

The bottom line is that parents have to teach siblings

to love each other and bond. It does not happen by force, directions nor osmosis. The heart loves not the eyes. Real bonding is the results of hard work and long and constant caring.

Do I regret not having a good strong male role model in their home? Yes, sometimes, but I exposed them to men and other women of great values and strong character, therefore they had exceptional role models. I am reminded of a standup comedian, who bragged about what a hard working and strong woman his mother of many children was, the comedian said, "Then you ain't half the man your momma was." I do not see myself as a perfect mother but I always knew I had to do twice as much work as mothers with good husbands who were also good fathers. God saw me through.

From my most profound point of view. "Life is worth living when you can die and leave the living in love with each other." Amen, Amen. Amen.

24

An Epilogue from the Big Brother's Point of View by Brian Tenell Flakes

Life does sometimes twist our fate. It seems to have overwhelmed me and left me stranded in a place that saved my life, the SAF P facility of the Texas Department of Corrections. I realized while I was there that I had made many choices that were not a part of my rapport of life skills. I realized that my mother and all of her resource people and events were designed for me to not end up in a SAF P facility. But, I also learned very well how to be a survivor. Therefore, I took every advantage of being in a protective environment to search my inner being and actively participate in the concepts of behavioral modification that the skilled and educated counselors offered to all of its clients. The next writing is an essay that I wrote while in the SAF P facility. My mother has kept it in order for me to use as good therapy while I count the one day at a time success of being sober and drug free.

My Life Story

CHILDHOOD: My childhood was filled with a lot of excitement and travel. Every summer we traveled on family vacations. Totaling twenty-seven different states all by car and beginning in Temple, Texas. My mother did all of the driving. I am the second child of three children and was reared by our single mother. I have one older sister and one younger brother with each I am still very close. My mother reared us with excellent parental skills. Instilling in us strong moral values, the value of education, proper etiquette of life and social skills. She taught us to be positive and goal oriented. She supported us in all our extra activities of school and in life. I was reared to be an active member in church at a early age. My mother did not allow sibling rivalry to exist in our home. She was never afraid to discipline me when I needed discipline but never in excess. As a child I normally made friends quickly and easily. Christmas was always a great time of year in our home. We always got a lot of luxury gifts. My grandmother played a very big part in my happiness as a child and an adult; for her nothing was too good for me. I have always been competitive in sports and games. I like winning.

At an early age, I was given opportunities to expand and develop my talents and skills that many of my friends could not afford. My childhood travels taught and showed me many things and an appreciation for what my mother gave all three of us. We visited dams, gorges, museums, aquariums, mints, caves, canyons, oceans, lakes, famous bridges, historical statutes, Disney Land, Disney World, and other things too numerous to remember. While traveling she took time for us to learn something about the different cultures of the people whom we had visited.

Poverty in Southside Chicago was frightening. I had never seen a child eat from a public trash can. We stood next to the fully dressed Native American, but we were terrified of their hatchets. We had been taught in school that all Indians would scalp us. My mother happily instructed us to stand beside the chief to take a picture.

Though trembling, we obeyed. Guess what? They did not bother us, and we learned they were civil from our own experience. My childhood was truly filled with fantastic memories and joy-filled moments. All to be credited to my mother, a loving, caring, and positive strong woman. Drugs, alcohol, and smoking were never allowed in our home.

EDUCATION: High school was a breeze, fun times, and good grades. Briefly I worked two part-time jobs while in school. Paper boy by morning and part-time stocker. I was proud of having my own money. I played some basketball and was a starter, but not the star. I was just the most exciting player on the team. I had a high school sweetheart who also became the mother of my son. She and I went to the prom together. I was well liked and maintained a 3.0 grade point average. I too, had my own little car, and that made me more popular. I really enjoyed high school. I tried to get high, smoke marijuana, just to be cool. I never really enjoyed being high, but peer pressure made me think I was cool. My younger brother enrolled me in one semester of Temple Junior College. Afterwards I had one year of college in Dallas where I was majoring in business technology. I was a very good student, considering the amount of time without attending classes. I was voted class president, in Dallas, based on a popularity contest. However, I met the challenge better than I thought I would. I was afraid to fail in front of my peers. I left school while in recovery from a random crime gunshot wound. After healing from the gunshot wound I have not returned, yet.

DRUG HISTORY: I used crack as a crutch, but, it only caused me to stumble and fall. My drug history has taken me places I never would have gone and left me there to suffer all alone. When I reflect on the history of my drug addiction, I realize that it has to be "HISTORY," the past. It represents wasted money, many lies, broken hearts, loneliness, disappointment, mental confusion, anguish and pain. My drug history must not repeat itself. I cannot stand anymore blues nor misery. My addiction was truly cunning, baffling and very powerful. It made me play tricks on my mind. It had total control over the directions of my life. I had become overwhelmed by its power. Drugs became the focal point of my life. I lost good jobs, nice cars, strained relationships, betrayed my family member's trust and love, got evicted from one apartment after the other. It kept me on the run. Drugs caused chaos and havoc far too long.

I feel the end is near. This struggle is finally over; it is a burden removed. I can see and breathe again. The reality of my drug addiction is that it cost me more than money and peace of mind. I allowed it to cost me some of the prime years of my life, and sometimes that brings me close to tears. I have so many unfulfilled dreams and unfulfilled goals. My addiction led me to a lot of self-destruction. I am now going to close the doors on my addiction and say to my devilish adversary of the past "CRACK, go straight to hell. Crack, I know that you will always try to return. But, each time be aware that I am prepared for an all-out fight. I will continue to win in the end."

PAST TREATMENT: Half-measures have availed me nothing. Past treatment for the sake of pleasing others felt good, but not fulfilling. I realize that I must do it for myself. Outpatient treatment meant just going through the motions. It meant just doing what the requirement of my probation ordered. I never let go absolutely. I never had a sponsor nor a home group. No relapse prevention requirements. Treatment has been all talk, with very little action, which has led to small steps of progress and only back to addiction. This opportunity of intensive therapy and the absence of drugs will truly be beneficial and rewarding. Hopefully leading to a deep happiness and inner peace. I feel very positive and excited about my future and living it drug-free. Past treatment was like wishful thinking. This time I am going to make sobriety an eternal reality.

INCARCERATION: Jails were never a part of my life plans, but neither was drug addiction. Now, I know, they work hand in hand. I view incarceration as a form of negative motivation, soul searching, leading to growth. I have seen so much madness and confusion in jails that they will last me a lifetime. I have also seen many injustices performed by the justice system. Now I recognize that justice is truly blind to both blacks and whites. Incarceration has made me a calloused person and I developed an unknown anger that has led me into becoming a defensive person. The stay in a SAF P facility has become the longest time of incarceration that I have experienced. I am expecting to regain my direction and focus in life again as a result of my incarceration. I refuse to let this period of time in my life be considered wasted. I will grow from my incarceration.

RELATIONSHIPS: Many a relationship has come and gone without remorse. My addiction was at the center of most of the separations. Family relationships have become an on-again and off-again cycle, based on my success in my life at the time. My family has never lost faith nor confidence in my ability to overcome my life-threatening addiction. They really know ME. The relationship that hurts me the most is that I am not the uncle that I should be and that my brother deserves for his children. I deeply love them, and I must make amends to my brother for not being there for his family and being a positive part of their lives. It hurts me to know that in the process of my addiction I made my mother feel as though she was a victim. My mother knows and understands that it was not intentional. Nevertheless, she still has so much love for me in her heart. Truly a mother's undying love at its very best. I am still greatly blessed in our relationship.

The relationship with my son is deeply troubling, for him. I am filled with guilt and remorse. I created a bond with him but not as a pure father-and-son relationship. In time I will tell him all about my whereabouts. I will tell him what happened, what went wrong in my life, and how I overcame it through a lot of hard work and desire to become a better person, again. I pray that he will understand. His mother, my high school sweetheart, is totally confused about my actions. I must make amends to her for my lack of financial support. I feel like a deadbeat dad.

My relationship with my sister is solid. She knows what has happened to me. She assures me that she will always be there for me. I believe her. I have forced my addictions on relationships, which turned out to ruin each of them. I am okay with that. I have never truly been in love. I was always unfaithful. I never felt a need for monogamy. My addiction brought on a very active sex life, with women I would not take home to my mother. They just filled the need for space and loneliness. They never were able to fill the emptiness in my heart. I may have too high of expectation for women. I always wanted the best for Mrs. Brian T. Flakes, but I haven't been at my best. I accept that, too.

RECOVERY: Maintaining a positive state of mind is a must if I have any hope of living life according to the recovery program of SAF P. I can see the light at the end of the tunnel. I can hear the whispers of hope. I can touch the joy of my drug-free future. A richer life awaits me. I look forward to living it.

—Brian T. Flakes
(TDCJ #993777)

Where do I go from here? I am convinced that the only way is up. I have spent enough down time to know that I refuse to repeat any of my past mistakes.

The Texas Rehabilitation Commission is affording me several opportunities to reverse my past pattern of living and choices. I have enrolled and completed commercial truck-driving school in early 1998. I am driving cross country. My mother has already asked, "Would the company allow a passenger, may I ride with you sometimes?" The answer to that is without a doubt, YES. Our healed relationship is better than when I was a child and a young adult; we have matured. We have gained a greater sense of value, love, and respect for each other, while I am healing.

I will make amends for the relationships that I strained while I was in the clutches of my addiction. Truck driving is allowing me to spend more quality time with myself and make me a better person for my brother, sister, son, nieces and nephew, as well my mother.

It is hard to imagine that life can get any better with my mother; she has stood in the gap each and every time I needed her support. She says that I really don't "Owe her," but my heart knows I must compensate her emotionally and physically for the many trials she has helped me to overcome.

The one thing that my mother has prayed for the most is that I will come home with my head unbowed. She has told me repeatedly that my past is no embarrassment for her sterling reputation in our home town of Temple, Texas. I am honored that she feels there is nothing that I can do that will take up her "Welcome Home" mat for me. I am ready to face Temple with my natural big effervescent smile and clean heart. She still has a lot of influence with young people in Temple, Texas, and I hope that my polished life will tell them to avoid the potholes of life that I have stumbled through. I hope they will listen to her and take heed of her love, care, concern, and wise counsel. She has much to offer and so freely gives.

Lastly, as we grew up, she befriended many youths. Youths came to our home to see her as much or more than they came to see all three of her children. Many of those youths were troubled and afraid. Many have made beautiful lives for themselves and enjoy meaningful professions and families that reflect her teachings. She never spent enough time with others to shortchange our needs for nurturing. She did all of this with one income and did not make GS-07 until my brother was in college. We have asked her, "How did you make us feel so rich physically and emotionally?" Her simple answers were being frugal, wise, and willing to sacrifice many of her needs, emotionally and physically, for our well-being. Now I understand why she loves eagles. She soars from peak to peak.

I deserve a better life than I have given me. How do I know that? I am the son of an eagle. My brother is proof that she swooped down and put us back in the nest as often as needed for us to learn how to fly on the strength of our own wings. When she could not find the food (life's answers) we needed, she repeatedly ripped the seam in her own belly and fed us until we could fly again. She has kept her nest in excellent repair for our return when the storm cloud raged against any or all three of us.

She is retired now but not tired. She still lifts us up at every corner of our needs. She knows and keeps us aware that she is a now our lifeboat, not our ocean liner. Charles Lwanga Buyondo, her first exchange son, a native of Uganda and citizen of Sweden, has been enjoying her parenting for the last five of six years of his life. He says there is nobody like his host mother, we agree with Charles. However, he said it well, with a simple little magnet on her refrigerator. It shows majestic mountains and beautiful skies far beyond tree branches, the view of a stern-eyed eagle. It reads: "Retirement: After climbing the mountain, you can now appreciate the beauty of the view." I don't know if those words are from some noted philosopher or not, but they certainly are applicable for our mother and that is from the warden's, brother's point of view.

My mother loved teaching us through well-chosen literary verse. The one that I love the most she wrote:

Wondering and Finding

As a little boy I gazed out the school window wondering,
What people were doing beyond the horizon and beyond
my knowing.
I wished to see far beyond the clouds,
To the places where other things and people abound.

As a little boy I traveled, for my mother to be pleased,
I saw enough things for my mind to be teased.
I read our books of faraway lands,
I learned of things I wanted to hold in my hands.

I had no way to plan my own destiny,
Life for a little boy was a real mystery.
I dreamt of the day that I would be free to roam,
Today the highways are my second home.

Life did not work in my favor,
Yet, I yearned for glitz and glamour to savor.
As a man, life gave me the right travel and things to
see,
I ran into life searching, to find the real me.

I met many weary travelers along my way,
Many with sad and frightful stories for every day.
I learned the glitz and glamour was not for real,

I met trials and troubles and people who'd steal.

I took a dip into the dungeons below,
I could not tell my mother, life had struck me a painful blow.
I rambled and struggled to take care of myself,
I played the hand I had, bad hands I was dealt.

I found myself in a lowly and tragic pit,
Filled with mire and an awful scent.
I hated for my mother to see what I had become,
I was not her little guy she raised in our home.

I hit the bottom and for my sins I had to pay,
My mother never failed me, she loved me anyway.
I found a method for my woes to reverse,
I changed my life before it got worse.

I have had my days of wondering,
And I have been blessed to experience, *my,* finding.
I have revamped my thoughts about life itself,
I had taken the wrong road and *now I am finding myself.*

My mother reared my brother, sister and me,
With her eagle mentality.
She taught us the difference in eagles from a buzzard and a crow,
Thank God for His finding me and allowing me to grow.

—© by Myrtle L. Captain
Inspired by Brian Tenell Flakes

25

An Epilogue from the Warden's Point of View by Garland KaZell Flakes

I count it a great joy being my mom, sister, and brother's baby and here is my point of view as I look from the bottom up. It must be remembered that I love being all of their baby.

In my growing up, my brother always encouraged me to do good no matter how poorly I thought I had done. The family knows I was no Little League football star, but my Big Brother worked with me for the kick, punt, and pass contest. Guess what? I won third place. It did not matter that there were only three participants in my age group. In my Big Brother's eyes, it was as great as if I had won first place. After all he was my coach. My Big Brother and I enjoyed playing together, and he always picked me for his team. He was making every attempt to bring out my best athletic abilities. Together, we did all the things brothers do—wrestle, argue, and keep secrets. The wrestling was probably the funniest, because my Big Brother was quick and he would always win. When I grew bigger and heavier than he was and could get my arms around him, you guessed it—I got a "draw" in one wrestling match. Since he still won, I thought, *"Boy, my Big Brother is smart."* In school my Big Brother excelled and had lots of friends. I could not hang around him and his friends. After all I was three years younger and was his little brother. However, in the neighborhood it was okay. There were lots of younger sisters and brothers and we all played together.

My sister was, and still is, a princess to me. Often her wrath came upon me, for some little brother mischievous deed that I did. After all, I am five years younger than she and I guess that is what little brothers are supposed to be, mischievous. With admiration and love I remember presenting her to society at the Delta Sigma Theta Sorority, Inc.'s Christmas Debutante ball. My mom made her a beautiful white gown. She was the Belle of the Ball. Her dress had yards of white satin and lace. There were ruffles and lace from her waist to the floor, and the back stood open with extra layers of ruffles and lace. The collar was shaped like a heart and streamed down her back. Her hair was pretty, and she walked like a princess.

I had the honor of presenting her to society and holding her hand as she took her full knee bent bow and received her applause from the audience. My Big Brother took her hand as her escort, and they danced away like a prince and a princess. I thought this must have been my mother's dream come true, because, she took two days off from work to make that beautiful gown and prepare for this august event. My sister was the prettiest girl at the ball, and we were suave, tall, and looked as handsome as Denzel Washington. Just imagine my mother having two teenage Denzels. Well, to others we may not have been Denzels. However, the look in our mother's eyes said she was exceptionally proud of her three "gems." She often called us "gems" when she lauded us with words of adoration, admiration, happiness, and love.

I was proud of my sister in the Miss Black Temple Pageants. She won first runner-up more often than anyone else. Nevertheless, she performed different talents each year. She ballet-danced, sang, did dramatic presentations and gymnastics routines. I admired her for being so talented. I got a special joy watching people applaud when she graced the stages with her many talents.

She got her first car at the age of fifteen, a cute little white Ford Falcon station wagon with a brown panel down the side. Actually she was too young to take driver's education. But all three of us needed transportation to school. Momma taught her to drive and cautioned her to be extremely careful while she sat tall enough for the police to not notice how young she was. Not many boys had a sister to take them to and from school and the other places that children liked to frequent. When she carried and came to get me, it made me feel very special and I delighted in her loving me as her baby brother.

My fondest thought of my sister was when I told her that I would be getting married. She cried tears of jubilation. Now, my joy comes when I see her enjoying being Aunt Trell to my children.

My momma—it is a fact that she is **awesome** in my eyes, and that is an understatement about her from my point of view. If I attempted to tell the "Rest of the story," as Paul Harvey would say, this book would never end.

As a young boy, I began to make choices about attending college. I had been introduced to manual labor. At the age of ten, our cousin Jimmie Flakes, Sr. fired me from his lawn-care team. I was happy to be fired. I learned early that working in the sun and heat was not how I wanted to earn a living. While in Texas Lutheran College in Seguin, Texas, some of the very rich and generous ranchers paid me to pitch hay. I did. Hay pitching reinforced that I did not like grit, grime, and sweat. The rancher' wives grilled some of the finest and largest steaks I have eaten; the steaks helped to make hay pitching bearable. However, my experiences with manual labor makes me unafraid of it, but I don't relish it on a permanent basis.

Academically, I studied and worked hard to fulfill my basketball obligations for my partial scholarship. I was a fierce Texas Lutheran College Bulldog, and my mother's ever-present presence made her become known as "Momma Dog."

In my senior year, 1985, I transferred to Huston-Tillotson College in Austin, Texas. On 22nd of December 1998, I got married and my Big Brother served as my best man. There was no other person whom I wanted to serve in that major role other than my Big Brother. His son was my ring bearer. My mother's eyes beamed as she looked at my Big Brother, my little four-year-old nephew, and me in our white tuxedo suits and me in tails. She held a loving and radiant permanent smile on her face. As I looked at my Big Brother and nephew, I knew they were the two most important men in my life. I still cherish their sharing that blessed event. I graduated from Huston-Tillotson College, Austin, Texas, in May of 1986.

My brother came from Dallas to share this special and blessed event in my life. My Big Brother was jubilant and happy over my graduation. His being happy for me meant a lot because I had wanted him to have graduated from college, three years before me. Nevertheless, he was as happy for me as if he had done so himself. My mother hosted my graduation party for dinner. Having my Big Brother and sister along with my wife and my mother's mentor, Mrs. B. Kay Hornsby, the Rev. A. C. Sutton, Texas NAACP President, and James Smith of San Antonio made this another great day of memory. My brother's happiness and presence was another exhibition of our special bond. I valued his presence.

Also, in May my first daughter, Brittany, was born. Now my brother and sister were an aunt and uncle. Brittany was special to them; they showed their love was a fact and that is not just from my point of view.

In June I went to work for the Texas Department of Corrections, Texas Department of Criminal Justice/Institutional Division. Since, my first job was in Huntsville, Texas, it afforded my wife an opportunity to return to college and graduate from Sam Houston State University. She also had an opportunity to work for the same agency. Going to work for the agency has been a blessing that only God could have provided.

On my very first day of employment, a female supervisor was killed by an inmate. Immediately, I realized that being killed was the ultimate sacrifice of my new employer. I started working as a Correctional Officer, which is the front line warfare of any penal institution. It can be associated with the manual labor level of a prison career. I am glad I had the experience of being an Correctional Officer because it has made a difference in how I see and appreciate the big picture of the Texas Department of Corrections Institution Division.

My career has many and varied occupational experiences. I worked in Necessities, in charge of personnel of the laundry facilities. I was promoted to Classification Specialist and later to Classification Chief. I enjoyed helping the system and inmates get the best from proper housing. One of the most significant positions that I held was Assistant Administrator in the "Operation Kick-it" Community Education Program. This position involved traveling and carrying inmates across the state of Texas.

The inmates and I spoke to thousands of Texas youths concerning their experiences in prison and how to avoid doing things that may lead to incarceration. The inmates accepted questions and provided answers designed to help reduce youth criminal activities. The Kick-It program still plays a major role in community education and has a profound effect on the future of young Texans.

I was promoted and reassigned to several different other positions, among them Chief of Classification. In that position, I had the pleasure and challenge of opening a new prison facility. That duty included but was not limited to supervisor of Classification Division for 2,250 inmates from other facilities, loading all of their health and prison records into the computer. I was responsible for and ensured that the offenders duty locations were compatible to work in food service, laundry services, and all other departments. I ensured their duty assignments would maintain a safe and secure facility. I took this role very seriously and accomplished the mission without an attempt for escape, no hurt to anyone, no harm or danger, nor loss of person or property. However, doing it successfully and having fed the inmates a hot meal on the second day gave me a personal sense of achievement in the behalf of the inmates and the Texas Department Correction, Institution Division. I value that opportunity because it was a history-making fete. I knew my brother would be very proud of my ability to do a good job and having the leadership ability to have others help in this massive undertaking. Our mother told Brian of this accomplishment, and he told her, "That's my baby." She felt proud of Brian's pride in my accomplishments, though he was still having difficulties with his life problems. Our bond stayed strong, no matter where life had taken us.

Later, being promoted to Assistant Warden on July 1, 1994 was a pivotal point in my career. It meant that not only was I educationally prepared but also that I had paid my dues and earned each rung of the career ladder.

I was also learning and becoming wiser about the consequences of poor decisions and welcoming every opportunity to talk with my brother about his making better choices. At no time in the progress of my career did I feel my big brother was any less than I nor did I ever love him less for the choices he made. I continued to pray for him and loved him more.

I worked smart and hard in each position leading to assistant warden. As an assistant warden, I was blessed to be under the tutelage of an outstanding and sharing senior warden, Tim West. I felt like a protégé of a master mentor. I knew that I could aspire to either become a senior warden or continue being the best assistant warden that my senior warden needed, deserved, and expected. I watched my senior warden do some great things for the prison system and the inmates. I knew that the best way to show my senior warden how much I appreciated his mentoring me and my career choices was to apply for and be promoted to a senior warden, too. In May 1997, I was promoted to senior warden of the Richard P. LeBlanc Pre-Release Substance Abuse Treatment Program. My unit emphasis is to help our clients modify their behavior and goals. We are to provide them tools to help them assimilate into free society and to become proud and productive citizens. That is how we help to reduce recidivism. I have made my commitments to behavioral modification clear to my total staff. I expect our clients to actively participate in the behavioral modification concepts of our program, so they will be more equipped to face the free society from a more optimistic point of view.

How does this relate to *The Warden and His Brother*? Very much. My love for my brother, despite his choices, has made me more conscious of the consequences of offenders who commit drug-related crimes. My big brother never committed a crime against another person nor property. He never trafficked, made, nor sold drugs. But that does not make him innocent of criminal acts against himself. Therefore, he too had to pay for his crimes against himself. My mother had a difficult time understanding how the drug world and this part of the judicial system works. I tried to help her understand; eventually she did. She probably will never see it from an institutional point of view, but she has learned that my brother's experience at the SAF P unit has helped to save his life. Her understanding is another one of my prayers answered.

Since my big brother's release, we have talked deeply many times. He has given me another point of view of the SAF P program. He encourages me to activate my best assets and attributes to my current position. Based on his experiences, I know that I work for the best division in the best agency in the corrections community. Again that it is my point of view.

Finale—from the Warden

Do I wish that I had chosen another career? No. I know some people hate prison systems and their personnel. Yet, people want a safe and crime free environment in which to live. Some people live on the borderline of violating the law and others by some twist of fate become inmates. Regardless of how they become inmates, I stay committed to proper administration of my unit, and to respect each man as a potential rehabilitated productive adult. If I treated anyone less than fair, I would be robbing him of the right to think he can become a positively changed person. My big brother still teaches me a lot of smart stuff. He objectively tells me how the system feels from the other side. I can trust what he says, because he wants me to continue becoming the best man and warden that I can become. But then, that is what big brothers do; that is my point of view. I am still looking from the bottom up. Let us not forget I am their baby.

Fatherhood is the most serious aspect of my life next to my service to God. My mother and I are much alike in this area. She took motherhood very seriously. Not having a father presented a serious challenge to me as a young father. I often questioned myself on appropriate timing for children's responsibility, training, nurturing, and rearing them from a man's point of view. The beauty of not having a father was that my mother was determined to expose us to all aspects of life and people of good character. I got a salad bowl of ministers, Mr. Fix-its, coaches, counselors, teachers, some of whom had taught my mother. I met and worked with civil rights leaders of different races, business people, high-level government, and public officials. She was very selective of those who were close enough to impress or impact on our maturation or become personal mentors. My well-selected mentors have helped me to stay in the middle of the road. Rev. Williamson said that "It is easier to move back or cross the road when you stand in its middle." To each of my mentors, I often express, "Thanks." A couple of my mentors have died, but their wisdom and respect lives in my mind and heart. On and from all my mentors, I still draw strength. Recently, God gave me a mentor who is near and dear to me, my former Senior Warden, Tim West. I had the distinct pleasure learning what a real and good warden should and must be in order to help change the lives of our offenders. Also, he introduced me to "Walk of Emmaus," one of my richest most rewarding experiences. He has also taught me more about the depth of fatherhood and what it really means. He and I share a lot things and time. He gives me wise counsel in many areas of life. We went to "Stand in the Gap" together. This too was a rewarding experience. It is my desire to be equally as resourceful with the employees of Richard P. LeBlanc. I thank God for our relationship, which is based on genuine friendship and trust.

Serving God, as my father, has freed my mind of a need for an earthly father. It is my opinion that men need to support each other and provide wise counsel while also holding each other accountable for our actions. I am sure God is pleased with my points of view on mentoring and friendship. He continues to bless me in my many different endeavors.

Fatherhood is coupled with being an uncle to my brother's son and my wife's nieces. I have learned that being an uncle is a serious responsibility, also. I have not had the privilege of being close to Keith KaZell, my brother's son, due to distance and location. I do have two nieces whom I get to see and keep more often. I recall my mother talking about Uncle Fuzzy and Uncle Jasper. Both of these men were very important to her, and she frequently took us to visit each of them. I hope to be as important to my nephew and nieces as my mother's uncles were to her. My nieces' parents claim that I spoil them. I claim to have my bluff over them. I know that they know I love them, and from my point of view, I have the best nephew and nieces any uncle could want.

The major question is, How did I deal with my brother being confined? I did not visit him because I know some offenders do not like offenders who have relatives working for the system. Some offenders can and will deliberately make their lives more difficult. As an assistant warden, I shared with my senior warden that my brother was sent to a SAF P facility. I was promoted to Senior Warden while he was in SAF P. I told my staff and offenders population that he was in a facility similar to what I serve as warden. Why did I tell of his misfortune? Experience has shown me that people find other's problems less interesting when persons have acknowledged their problems themselves. I supported my brother's stay in the SAF P facility by writing to him often. I prayed for him and kept our mother's spirit positive about his recovery.

For his thirty-seventh birthday, I deposited into his account \$37.37. The 37/37 was an analogy for him to think twice about his station in life at the age of thirty-seven. Many days I wished to see him face to face, to hug him, and to look into his eyes. The last time I saw him was on December 25, 1991 at the waiting for the birth of my son. Since his release, when I talk to him, he sounds SUPER. His voice is vibrant, his thinking is clear, and he seems to be on track. The bigger part of me stayed focused on the fact that he is my Big Brother and I have and will always love him, despite his choices. I realize that he has made some decisions with some negative consequences, for which he accepted and paid his dues. My Big Brother is still smart and has come to realize that life is a different kind of wrestling match and the odds have a higher percentage of losses and draws. He and I know how we feel about each other. After all we are brothers and brothers keep secrets.

I have not told my children where their uncle has been, though at times they have expressed hope to see him. Though they have never asked, I think they have surmised his whereabouts. Being the kind of man he is, I believe that in time he will explain where he was and how and why not to make bad decisions as he made. Recently, he talks to them on the telephone and they displayed joy for hearing his voice. How could that happen?

I'm sure they love my big brother in absentia because they hear me express that I love my big brother. They can sense the strong and loving bond that exists between their dad and his brother. My wife was a source of strength and a sounding board, during my brother's presence in SAF P. She helped me to not let my personal life spill into my professional life. She encouraged me to stay focused on my career. I have stayed focused; however, it is only natural that man will adopt some of anything that is good, regardless from which source it comes.

During my brother's dark days, my mother "stood in the gap" for us. Our mother serves as the connecting link between us. She said that she felt our bond while I was in her womb and Brian boldly protected our image to a nasty neighbor. I have helped her to defend Brian and herself to people who asked silly questions and express their many different assumptions. I have also, learned that my mom's visit to other prison units have made a impact on how she sees the Institution Division of the prison system. More importantly, she expressed an understanding concept that a SAF P facility is much different than the hard-core criminal units. I felt good when she told me that her heart screamed out, "Lord, please don't let my son become an inmate."

I have talked with her many different times about some of the intricacies of criminal justice and the Institution Division. I don't really know what she thought of those conversations, but apparently they went well because she expresses her understanding of the world of drug addiction. She is verbal and believes in open two-way communications. If she had problems with our system, she would have stated her concerns. I know that she is proud of my role as a warden and has always said that I am compassionate. However, I watched and learned a lot from her and her civil rights endeavors and as a tough decision maker in her different roles at Fort Hood. She has made final decisions that impacted the lives of many employees. She has said to me many times, "I (she) snatch and stab them while you (me) patiently pierce them; either way they are dead." When she has repeated that statement, it was always when a tough, hard decision had to be made in the interest of fairness and justice. She does not believe in rolling over and playing dead; neither do I. She is a strong advocate for fairness and so am I. I am sure being her baby has a lot to do with my life.

The next major question is, Were you ever inclined to request special treatment for your brother? The answer is

NO. After all, he kept teaching me to be responsible and to be held accountable for our actions, whether good or bad. He continued to encourage me to keep forging ahead in my career. He never expected me to do anything illegal while he continued to advocate that I do right, all the time. Brian knows that we were reared to respect fairness and consistency. From my professional point of view, I make Yes and No decisions that will apply to all 1,000 offenders in my unit. If one offender gets a NO for all the right and fair reasons, all other 999 offenders or staff members deserve the same YES or NO, as it applies. I have learned that no one can consistently read nor think between the lines; therefore I make decisions based on what is on the line. My brother never asked for special treatment and was never on a unit for which I have worked; therefore that issue is a moot point.

How do I manage now? Nothing has changed. I still make fair Yes and No decisions consistently. The SAF P program in my unit is working very well. The staff knows my commitment to the program as well as my expectations. I have a burning desire to help our agency maximize the state's funding, to reduce recidivism, and to restore clients to positive and productive citizens.

As it relates to my brother and me, where do we go from here? He is still my big brother and I love him deeply. I look forward to giving him a hug and a Holy kiss. I want to see him face-to-face and to join the winners circle by encouraging other baby brothers to stay on the right track and to make good choices in order to avoid the consequences that are inherent with making poor decisions. He can do that very well; he is my big brother and that is the point of view from the eyes of his big little brother. We are sons of an eagle.

Throughout my career, many staff members have

asked me, how can I be a Christian and work as a Senior Warden in the Institution Division. My usual response is, "Christians have to earn a living, too." However, I know Christians and other believers employed in the system have helped systematically. There is a saying at some units, "Welcome to the gates of hell." I immediately pledged to stop that kind of mentality because actually we are the offenders' doors to freedom. Our offenders are usually within six months of exiting the prison system and are paying their last installment for the crime they have committed. I want each client to look back at the Richard P. LeBlanc Unit and look forward to life with a Rev. Dr. Martin Luther King, Jr. mentality: "Free at last, free at last, thank God Almighty, I am free at last." It is also said that it is hard to soar with eagles and live with buzzards. I expect the Richard P. LeBlanc Unit to be a mountaintop experience and the offenders will soar away as eagles, run and not get weary nor faint. In my mother's most recent travels, she wrote and forwarded to me one of the most inspirational poems that I have read. It is titled *Reasons.* It is dedicated to the inmates, clients, and offenders of Texas Department of Criminal Justice and the youth of our society.

Reasons

There are no reasons for me not to dream,
There are no reasons for me to not wish for things.
There are reasons for me to think while walking by a
 water stream,
There are reasons for me to think I will accomplish
 things.

There are no reasons for me to feel left out,
There are no reasons for me to feel self doubt.
There are reasons for me to seek change,
There are reasons why I should expect change.

There are no reasons why I should not try with all my
 might
There are no reasons for me to not have vision and
 foresight.
There are reasons why the I should venture and
 explore,
There are reasons why the world has an open door.

There are no reasons why I should not peak the sky,
There are no reasons why I cannot soar the sky.
There are reasons why I should succeed,
I have the potential of any seed.

There will always be reasons why I should be
The best of all that I can be, you'll see.
My reasons are because I am free,
Just to be me.

© by Myrtle L. Captain
Inspired by Warden Garland KaZell Flakes

Our united prayer is that *The Warden and His Brother, from Their Mother's Point of View* will serve as an inspiration to help make life happier and more prosperous for others.

My brother's success since release from the SAF P program has broadened my point of view in behavior modification. He is enjoying a drug free life and doing what he always wanted to do, driving big trucks. He visits my family and my son sees him as the best Uncle Brian a kid could have. I see our offenders as men that I must help to modify their behavior and return them to a free society with no desire to return to the TDC and gain some life skills to support their freedom.

I am committed to ensuring our offenders take advantage of the programs that are available. I am anxious to add other incentives for our offenders to want education and to improve their life skills. Some of the offenders in my unit say that I am different in that I truly care and show my concern for their well-being. Part of that was always the hope I had for my brother. Now that I have seen my brother come to the end of the road of self-destruction and turn around, I know that I can help our men in the Richard P. LeBlanc unit to do the same. For Texas, I will do what I want to do, "Give Texas back their sons, fathers, husbands, etc. in better health than when they came to TDC."

The Warden and His Brother, from Their Mother's Point of View is more than an account of my brother and my shared love and bond. It is about hope and recovery from a series of bad decisions that leads to incarceration. It is about hope for people who have experienced many different kinds of problems in life. It is about my mother being a strong little girl who learned how to find options and build on her strengths and never let obstacles deter her dreams. It is about the strange love of a grandmother who did not know how damaging her actions were upon her daughter and her family. It is about our sister remaining the princess to her brothers and her being special to each family member in her own special way. It is about an Uncle that never offered anything positive to his sister nor her family, but has always been respected as an Uncle by his niece and nephews.

The Warden and His Brother, from Their Mother's Point of View is also about a community that served as a positive reinforcement for single mothers who tried to rear children who deserved some of the benefits of society and a right to formal education and occupations that afford them the right to earn the American dream. In all of its lessons there is something that can benefit any reader and offer some resolution for many problems that come with life.

The primary family focused in *The Warden and His Brother, from Their Mother's Point of View* is also a family that is still growing. Each of its members has grown tremendously with this writing and is more willing to share with others the fruits of believing in oneself, trusting and believing in God and sharing a bond between each other that cannot be broken. Each member is respected for their own choices in life.